I0172958

THE WAY
OF
ESCAPE

THESE THINGS
Second Edition

JEWELINE R. ANDREWS

Katrina'sWORKS
P U B L I S H I N G

No part of this book may be used or reproduced in any matter without permission, except in the case of brief quotations embodied in articles or reviews.

All rights are reserved by the author.

ISBN-978-0692555903
ISBN-0692555900

**The Way of Escape
These Things**

**Copyright © October 2015
Jeweline R. Andrews**

Edited by Katrina Avant

**Cover Design
Soul Sister Ink
K a t r i n a s w o r k s . c o m**

Table of Contents

Foreword

"Looking to Jesus, the author and finisher of our faith, who for the joy that was set before Him endured the cross despising the shame has sat down at the right hand of the throne of God." (**Hebrews 12:2.**)

Indescribably, His blessings are more than I can describe. For example: "God, who at various times and in varies ways spoke in times past to the fathers by the prophets has in these last days spoken to us by His Son, whom He has appointed heir of all things through whom also He made the worlds." revealed in Hebrews **1:1-2**.

One day while sitting in my doctor's office, a lady excitedly shared her personal testimony with me. She said God told her He wanted her to be His witness. She responded, LORD I know You couldn't be talking to me I am sixty years old now. God responded, I've been talking to you a long time but you just weren't listening to Me.

The woman and I shouted excitedly together right there in that office! Jesus Christ, "Who is the brightness of His glory," see verse **3a.**

As for me, I will add in my second edition of this book, blessed by God ,to record chapters and verses instead of abbreviations manifested to me according to great feedback some of my dear readers questioned. So to make it plain to us, the letter v reveals verse, vv, two verses I wrote these things throughout my book. I thank God for; The Holy Spirit our infinite precious Helper is at work in my life. He who is, "The express image of His person and upholds all things by the Word of His power when He had, by Himself purged our sins and sat down on the right hand of the Majesty on high," (**verse 3b.**)

Amazingly a description in brightness describes Jesus Christ; "Being made so much better than the angels, as He has by inheritance obtained a more excellent name than they," (**verse 4**.)

God called my name Jeweline R. Andrews in 1985 and said, I want you to be My sanctified witness in the streets of West Memphis Arkansas, my hometown. God increased my confidence by amazingly revealing the brightness of His glory to someone like me He says. "Fear not, for I have redeemed you. I have called you by name: You are Mine. When you pass through the waters I will be with you. And through the rivers they shall not overflow you: When you walk through the fire you shall not be burned, nor shall the flame scorch you: For I AM the LORD your God, the Holy One of Israel; your Savior." (**Isaiah 43:1b-3a)**

This scripture in Isaiah purposely justifies God's plan of safety. He purposely chose others to witness together by His power. We prayed and witnessed together twenty years; weather permitted once a week in every direction of the compass; north, east, south and west.

God said: "I gave Egypt for your ransom, Ethiopia and Seba in your place. Since you were precious in My sight, You have been honored and I have loved you; Therefore I will give men for you, and people for your life." (**vv 3b-4**.) God promised four great things, "Fear not, for I will be with you; I will bring your descendants from the east, and gather you from the west," (**verse 5**.) And I believe Him.

God preciously increased His blessings in likeness of a family affair, purposely saying: "I will say to the north, Give them up. And to the south do not keep them back! Bring My sons and My daughters from the ends of the earth: Everyone who is called by My name, Whom I have created for My glory; I have formed him, yes, I have made him. Bring out the blind people who have eyes and the deaf that have ears," **verses 6-8 revealed within the same chapter**. I'm so excited that I can hear, the Holy Spirit talking to me, and my desire is to do what God says to me.

Justified in God, we lead souls to Christ by the breath of the inspiration of our God Almighty. A pastor chosen to preach the gospel many years ago in our hometown, revealed his innermost desire to see miracles in action. He provided an increase to the place God sent him to preach the gospel to His people, manifested in **Isaiah 61:1-3**, and the place where Jesus taught, **Luke 4:18**.

Throughout our land, many people remain in intensive hospital units, nursing homes and are even home bound due to illness in hope of miracle healings. But God is faithful, because Obama care is available to many poor outcast people, so have faith in God and invest in it. Since States may rename health insurances such as: Family Healthcare U.S.A., America Rescue Act, for example. "Medicare for All," even the sick, and homeless may be able to invest in a plan giving a chance for God's mercies to hide so many miseries. A song writer penned, I believe, titled, "I Want to Be Your Sanctified Witness" I believe in 1985, God affirmed my call to be His sanctified witness, and the same year we purchased our home. And the same year, I was hired by a service action agency; East Central Arkansas Economic Development Corp. in Forrest City Arkansas.

Isaiah declared, "Let all the nations be gathered together, let all people be assembled; who among them can declare this and show us former things? Let them bring forth their witnesses that they may be justified or let them say it is truth." **Isaiah 43:9,** I rewrite the Word is truth.

Amazingly in God I trust, we are free to make right choices since He declares great and mighty things on earth with amazing reminders such as it is recorded, saying; "You are My witnesses said the LORD: And My servant whom I have chosen, that you may know and believe Me and understand that I AM He. Before Me there was no God formed after Me." (**Isaiah 43:10**.)

 An elderly retired pastor would always repeat his testimony whenever I greeted him in the marketplace. Because I would always ask him how was he doing? He would always answer: "I've never done better in my life." He was a precious witness for our God; retired yet not tired at all. He always purchased beef short ribs according to his taste. The old pastor passed away one day; but his testimony continues to live onward in sweet memory may God rest his soul.

I write of hall of fame blessings. God declared, "I, even I, AM the LORD, and besides Me there is no Savior I have declared and saved, I have proclaimed, And there was no foreign god among you; Therefore you are My witness, Says the LORD." (**verses 11-12.**)

Graciously one day I shared the old pastor's testimony with one of my home bound former sick classmates and he did not forget the old pastor' true story; amazingly before I opened my mouth he said, "I've never done better in my life." So I pass on the words of Jesus; He said: "Sanctify them through Your truth: Your Word is truth," (**John 17:17.**)

Lovingly, I greet my entire family, immediate and extended; along with friends and whosoever will read my God given book. And in sweet memories, I also want to acknowledge our deceased family members. I would also like to extend God's blessings to all alumni and staff who attended and taught at our precious Wonder High School, *Home of the Lions.* It is an honor to someone like me to make mention of **Wonder**'s best fame in Him.

Dedication to Wonder High School Class of 1961

Greetings to my special former classmates of 1961; I cite our class Motto: "Less than our best is Failure:" Colors Sky Blue & Navy Blue.

It is a pleasure to invite former staff and attendees to **Wonder**'s gatherings every Memorial Day weekend. Our school of yesteryears is known to us today, as Wonder Elementary and Wonder Junior High, located on the south-side; down by the railroad tracts in West Memphis Arkansas. In memory of all deceased staff, all former classmates, my special classmate and twin brother J.K. Robinson Jr., our only dear brother; our school colors, "Black & Gold" and our ALMA MATER. I quote our precious song, in which remains a celebrated wonder in Him:

"Wonder High School, Wonder High School, Wonder High School, Bless her name! Whether in defeat or victory we will love her just the same. So we cheer for Wonder High School 'tis for her we will fight for fame and we'll sing her praises down in every lane. Wonder High School Bless her name."

The best is yet to come, God said: "Behold, I will do a new thing; now it shall spring forth; shall you not know it? I will make a road in the wilderness and rivers in the desert." (**Isaiah 43:19**.) Hallelujah to our God always.

Undefeated and blessed abundantly by God in Christ, Mr. Barack H. Obama was elected 44th President of the United States of America; first and second terms from 2009 through 2016. May he have the peace of God within him and of Him. Also to the First Lady, Mrs. Michelle Obama and first daughters; Mr. Joe Biden, chosen Vice President of this country; Dr. Jill Biden, his wife, their staff, volunteers, and all Americans and nations, may the peace of God abide within and outward. His golden rule unites us. Jesus said: "Just as you want men to do to you, do you also to them likewise." (**Luke 6:31.**)

As I dedicate my book, and send out an invitation that whosoever will read these things in reverences to God's great and mighty blessings, certainly we have His Word continuously.

Chapter One
"These Things Two Ways"

"The blessing of the LORD, it makes rich and He adds no sorrow with it," **Proverbs 10:22**.

 These things captured my attention; stirred up my spirit with the joy of the LORD, from the crown of my head to the soles of my feet inwardly and outwardly.

A few years ago, God-breathed in my spirit to write a book and to investigate His blessings and divine relief aid in favor of His blessings. I am constantly inspired and in awe to the core of my soul. Blessed, knowing His voice, I accepted the awesome invitation within my God given heart, soul and mind, wondering: where do I go from this place. I am constantly in awe in Him.

It's not just my God given imagination. This blessing has encompassed me a very long time. Because I rely on great things in Him, I imagine even this very day and hour many words enter my ears to and fro. But God declared it saying,

> "Indeed, before the day was, I AM He; and there is none that can deliver out of My hand: I work, and who will reverse it?" **Isaiah 43:13**.

Today I know why our ancestors talked to themselves when they thought no one was watching. It was because, whenever they thought things were too hard, God spoke a Word from above. And when the answers came, they heard these words say.

> "In that hour Jesus rejoiced in Spirit and said, I thank You, Father, LORD of heaven and earth that You have hid-den these things from the wise and prudent and revealed these things to babes: Even so, Father, for it seemed good in your sight." **Luke 10:21**.

In that very hour, Christ is God's number One praise Leader; always declaring:

> "All things have been delivered to Me by My Father, and no one knows who the Son is except the Father and who the Father is except the Son, and the one to whom the Son wills to reveal Him" **Verse 22**.

I confess today; rejoicing in God who breathes life in all living things. I offer shout outs to Him, for special changes in the United States of America, as He uses Mr. Obama and Mr. Biden, according to his glory. Focusing on Him, we are blessed of the LORD.

So I pray for peace instead of war, because where there is peace, war is absent absolutely.

"Then He turned to His disciples and said:

> Blessed are the eyes which see the things you see: For I tell you that many prophets and kings have desired to see what you see and have not seen them; what you hear and have not heard it." **Verses 23-24**

Anonymously, I make mention of people in my book, alive or otherwise. True blessings God revealed to me in private and in public. He is apt to know what shoes fit our feet since He knows all names, past, present and future. An example of this can be found here:

> "A certain lawyer stood up and tested Him saying, Teacher what shall I do to inherit eternal life? And He said to him: What is written in the law? What is your reading of it?" **Verses 25-26**

Jesus revealed His heart on purpose to this unnamed lawyer, because, he answered his own double questions right back saying:

> "You shall love the LORD your God with all your heart, and with all your soul, and with all your strength, and with all, your mind and your neighbor as yourself. And He said to him: You have answered rightly: do this and you will live," revealed in verses **27-28**.

Jesus cleared the lawyer's record manifested in the New Testament saying: "You shall love the LORD God with all your heart," a taste of **Matthew 22:37a**.

> "But he, willing to justify himself, said to Jesus, and who is my neighbor? Then Jesus answering and said, a certain man went down from Jerusalem to Jericho, and fell among thieves who stripped him of his cloths wounded him and departed, leaving him half dead," **Luke 10:29-30**:

Jesus knew his thoughts and tested him.

> "Then Jesus answering and said: now by chance a certain priest came down that road: and when he saw him, he passed on by on the other side.

Likewise a Levite, when he arrived at the place came and looked, and passed on by on the other side." **Verses 31-32**

Amazed, reality clicked in. Jesus illustrated two-way examples, good verses bad. Revealed, His doer's works are rarely noticed on earth. Yet we find today the parables of Jesus reveal wisdom from above and He passed on great things we should know and practice likewise.

"But a certain Samaritan, as he journeyed, came where he was: when he saw him he had compassion on him. So he went to him, and bandaged his wounds, pouring oil and wine, set him on his own beast, and took him to an inn, and took care of him." verses **33-34**

Awesomely, Jesus revealed a way to reach another level.

"On the next day when he departed he took out two pence and gave to the innkeeper and said take care of him; and what-ever more you spend when I come back again, I will repay you: So which of the three do you think was neighbor to him who fell among thieves?" see verses **35-36**.

Because questions arise daily; often answers are available in likeness as it is written awesomely saying;

"And he said, He who showed mercy on him, then Jesus said to him, Go do likewise." **Verse 37**

Words of God show us how very much He pities us always since neither believers nor unbelievers are able to breathe,

His breath of life without power from His Spirit of life in that is purified truth. However, Martha and Mary were Jesus' true friends and today we continue to talk about these two sisters. They were complete opposites, yet Jesus didn't blame Martha who showed her love to Him in a different way. They were different people leaving no need for jealous.

> "Now it happened as they went that He entered a certain village; and a certain woman named Martha welcomed Him into her house. And she had a sister called Mary, who sat at His feet, and heard His Word: But Martha was distracted with much serving, and she approached Him and said, LORD, do You care that my sister has left me to serve alone?" **Verses 38-40a**

By observing the character of the two sisters, the same thing happens today. My sincerest hope is to practice and imitate Jesus, since Good Samaritans work to please Him. Martha spoke out and said:

> "Therefore tell her to help me," **Verse 40b**.

> "And Jesus answered said to her, Martha, Martha; you are careful and troubled about many things: But one thing is needful; and Mary has chosen that good part which shall not be taken away." **Verse 41-42**.

So when I think of these things, the gospel of Christ reveal believers and unbelievers are free to make choices. And Jesus reveals to us, a way to escape jealousy by the power of His Word and depending on Him. John recorded:

> "It was that Mary who anointed the LORD with fragment oil and wiped His feet with her hair,

whose brother Lazarus was sick," John 11:2; and he
also recorded: "Now Jesus loved Martha and her
sister; and Lazarus." **Verse 5**

John 11:1-45, is an absolute must read. I truly believe it to
be a way to escape envy.

Amazingly, the gospel writers of Christ reveal a good
Samarian's favor. But some did not mention the woman's
name in reference to her great works in Him. But I believe
her shoes fit her feet, for she walked and talked God's
truth, although certain people made a case against her.

> "But Jesus said, Let her alone; why trouble her?
> She has done a good work for Me. For you have
> the poor with you always, and whenever you wish
> you may do them good, but Me you do not have
> always. She has done what she could," **Mark 14:6-
> 8a**.

Jesus humanized a woman with multitudes watching, and
then He said:

> "She has come beforehand to anoint My body for
> burial. Assuredly, I say to you wherever this
> gospel is preached in the whole world what this
> women has done will also be told as a memorial to
> her." **Verse 8b-9**.

Jesus made it plain; it is no secret the pitiable treatment of
the poor of the land within the Old and New Testament
reveal these great and mighty blessings, and I believe
God's Word.

Moses recorded a debt-free release that remains in force from His Word and the evidence, I believe, reassures us of God's release saying:

> "At the end of every seven years you shall grant a release of debts. And this is the form of release: Every creditor who has lent anything to his neighbor shall release it; he shall not require it of his neighbor or his brother, because it is the LORD'S release," **Deuteronomy 15:1-2**.

God's lawgiver, leader, deliverer and prophet of Israel, behaved himself wisely in Him; (**see verses 3-4**). MOSES reminded people in his generation, and all generations to remember the poor it is recorded in His Word saying:

> "Only if you carefully obey the voice of the LORD your God, to observe with care all these commandments which I command you today. For the LORD your God will bless you just as He promised you; you shall lend to many nations, but you shall not borrow; you shall reign over many nation, but they shall not reign over you." Verses **5-6**

Then it happened; in honor to God, in my writings love and happiness met together in adoration. And I do adore Him. Moses legendarily wrote many instructions aimed especially to help care for the poor and outcast people of land, if it was not so I would not rewrite these things say:

> "If there is among you a poor man of your brethren, within any of the gates in your land which the LORD your God is giving you, you shall not harden your heart nor shut your hand from your poor

> brother, but you shall opened your hand wide to him and willingly lend him sufficient for his need, whatever he needs." **Verses 7-8, see verses 9-10**.

Moses recorded the results sufficiently, I believe just like God breathe in his spirit he wrote:

> "For the poor will never cease from the land; therefore I command you, saying: You shall open your hand wide to your brother, to your poor and needy in your land." **Verse 11** is indeed excellent examples to pass on!

For the cause, Congress is made up of men and women elected by citizens of the United States, who are in amazing positions to work for the people. Saved or unsaved, congressmen and women are paid great wages with good benefits as lawmakers today should work and earn their pay. Notably they hold power and duty to write laws worthy of our president's signature to sign into law to aid citizens within the U.S. Here are just a few of such topics involving laws: healthcare, immigration, gun control, housing, wage increases, Social Security and Medicaid. Moses had a great position, he wrote laws spoken to him by God. For examples looking back,

> "Moses began to explain this law saying, The LORD our God spoke to us in Horeb, saying. You have been in this place long enough at this mountain," **Deuteronomy 1:5b-6. See verses 7-8.**

And yet I believe as a Christian woman of faith, I've been in this place too long. But I found writing these things are apt to help me to procure, with the evidence to obtain and move on; just do what God says to me effectively from Him.

A question remains: Have our leaders in Congress been in these positions too long? Saying, no to all the above issues to aid all citizens seated in the hall of fame highest places? Moses wrote:

> "And I spoke to you at that time saying; I alone am not able to bear you. The LORD your God has multiplied you a thousand times the more numerous than you are and bless you as He has promise you. How can I alone bear your problems and your burdens and your complaints?" **verses 9-12**

The number one Question seems to be, how on earth can President Obama and his administration work all these things out without impartiality? That is to be fair according to all the above seen in v**erses 16-17**. I aim to write my second book by the power of God in Christ within me. And invest in these verses above like a charge to keep He gave me it is not over so be it. Because there are those who earn minimum wages, wages at a level less than living wages, with less benefits troubles me greatly, as a citizen of these United States, who has worked fifty years below poverty level opts outward within these great fifty-two States of America. My great hope, "In God we trust," shows on our money. We can't go backwards so we must go forward to prosper. I stick to God's great and mighty blessings as promised to anyone who believes Him.

For it is true, foreigners are plentiful among us today, in that were in trouble in America years before President Obama and V.P. Biden were leaders of this country. In which tells of all of us. For example, Luke, the great physician, I believe was a Gentile, he revealed Jesus' love for all people as it is written, He had no respect of persons glory hallelujah it is abundantly true.

> Because, "A woman in the city who was a sinner when she knew it was Jesus sat at the table in the Pharisee's house, brought an alabaster flask of oil," **Luke 7:37**.

God's writers penned absolutely wonderful work, justified in Him. John recorded again in wonder, to be continually manifested. **(See John 12:1-8).** For in these examples we can trust God and rely as recorded within the New and Old Testaments, I believe and trust Him.

> "Now a great many of the Jews knew that He was there; and they came, not for Jesus' sake only, but that they might also see Lazarus, whom he had raised from the dead." Verse 9 shows His acts and works are abundantly clear to me and I rewrite what happened saying. "But the chief priests plotted to put Lazarus to death also, because on account of him, many of the Jews went away and believed in Jesus:" **verses 10-11**.

I search God's Word daily; reviewing His amazing treasure chest, because the Word is out, in which manifest love, grace and mercy which reveal the greatness of salvation. As for me, envy does not work rightly in my spirit, and I owe it all to Christ, the anointed Specialist of God, as for me, influenced by the Holy Spirit, for example. A certain Senator reported 'no one gets rich alone.' I add not even inheritors. It was poor people who built the White House.

Same as with the Tower of Babel because they agreed with each other whether right or wrong and said:

> "Come, let us build ourselves a city and a tower whose top is in the heavens," **Genesis 11:4b**. But then Jesus said. "Blessed are you poor, for yours is the kingdom of God." **Luke 6:20b.**

So money is needful on earth, because we will not need money in heaven to spend. Money is marked, with words that always make me know it is absolute true for someone like me says. "In God We Trust. Silver and gold can be easily traded in for cash money since the United States makes money easily. Therefore the question is: what is greater, a lover of money or poor, homeless, hungry citizens of many races? Paul wrote:

> "For the love of money is a root of all kinds of evil, for which some have strayed from the faith in their greediness, and pierced themselves through with many sorrows," **1st Timothy 6:10**

> Whereas in Him five words reveals my title says in one awesome verse:

> "These things command and teach." 1st Timothy **4:11**

God is the glory; He spoke to me, and I rewrite what great things Jesus said to the world:

> "But seek ye first the kingdom of God and His righteousness and all these things shall be added to you." **Matthew 6:33**.

A cousin of mine said years ago, one could be homeless in three months. Today it's easy to figure the math, homeowner or renter, yet God said to me, stick to His blessings. So then, a man on cable television got it right when he said 'rent is too high, it has to be paid'. In memory, an elder lady reminded us that Paul visited Moses' law saying:

> "For it is written in the Law of Moses you shall not muzzle an ox while it treads out the grain." Is it oxen God is concerned about? Or does He say it altogether for our sakes? For our sakes no doubt, this is written that "he who plows should plow in hope, and he that threshes in hope should be partaker of hope." **1st Corinthians 9:9-10**.

Once, an elder in the choir sang a song entitled, I believe, "I Feel like Running". This very song today refreshes my spirit whenever she sings it. Young or old, it is written we reap what we sow, and I did not make up these precious words. I feel good shouting and running around my house praising God with all that is within me. It is so that He alone knows my heart, soul and mind; so be it.

> "If we have sown spiritual things for you, is it a great thing if we reap your material things? If others are partakers of this right over you, are we not even more? Nevertheless we have not used this right, but endued all things lest we hinder the gospel of Christ." **Verses 11-12**

More of the gospel of Christ is the key to good news; to read daily; to run to Him saying,

> "Do you not know that those who run in a race all run, but one receives the prize? And everyone who competes for the prize is temperate in all things. Now they do it to obtain a perishable crown, but we have an imperishable crown." **Verses 24-25 here is what I do daily,** I struggle to win the race on earth, because even at our old school of "Wonder" I ran on the tract team even in elementary and moved on the Junior high school was an excellent beginning, I'm not boasting on self, but celebrating Him continuously, because I can still run at seventy-three years old same as do many elders do today, if fact I won a few metals while working the three-county senior citizens, I bless His name likewise.

> "Therefore I run thus: not with uncertainty; thus I fight; not as one who beat the air." **Verse 26**

Paul explained to us a way to win metals on earth. First of all he writes, and I copy what he says:

> "But I discipline my body, and bring it into subjection lest when I have preached to others: I myself should become disqualified." **verse 27.**

In God, Paul was temperate. He characterized a sound view in the epistles of Christ. He made it clear to all who read these things; whatever one does good or bad, the same thing returns to us. So my thing is to run to win the race with joy, because I acknowledged a vow to God, but He revealed the vow to me from His Word. In the name of Jesus, I'm constantly disciplining self to just do what he says and He knows it is true. I rewrite great and mighty things below again;

"In God we trust." Abundantly in Him joy lingers on past midnight. For example, one of my prayer partners felt down before midnight. Then our mission president asked us to stand up and read a Psalm. My prayer partner read one of my favorites. That night she quietly read as written:

> "Oh, give thanks to the LORD, for He is good! For His mercy endures forever. Oh, give thanks to the God of gods! For His mercy endures forever. Oh, give thanks to the LORD of lords! To Him who alone does great wonders, for His mercy endures forever." **Psalm 136:1-4**

It's okay to feel down in spirit at times. Sometimes little children cry out to their fathers when they fall down and hurt themselves. In pity the psalmist said:

> "For His mercy endures forever; To Him who laid out the earth above the waters. For His mercy endures forever; To Him who made great lights, for His mercy endures forever; The sun to rule by day; For His mercy endures forever; the moon and the stars to rule by night; For His mercy endues forever," **verses 5b-9**.

Exceedingly the joy of the LORD leaped in my spirit abundantly.

> "Who remembered us in our lowly state, for His mercy endues forever." **Verse 23**

***

Greatly, the wondrous song continues because I know all verses and fact checked. These things,

> "For His mercy endures forever. And rescued us from our enemies, for His mercy endures forever: Who gives food to all flesh, for His mercy endues forever." **verses 24-25**.

I felt real good wrapped up and tied up in God's amazing love; seated in great company smiling; so glad to witness. It is a habit of mine that became habitual. When a woman of faith asked me what's up? I meditated on these things by faith in God's mercies thinking she knew my true stories. But a certain verse a song writer penned helps express my true story says: "I don't believe, He brought me this far to leave me now." I will write just a taste of what happened.

I was headed home from work one day from Forrest City, Arkansas. I fell asleep on the expressway, with the cruise set on seventy miles an hour, the speed limit. Suddenly, God awakened me in the middle of the medium. In a divine response He said, "Do not hit your brakes!" I heard Him, and looked around there were no vehicles in sight on the expressway. I was amazed, because traffic-wise, 5:00 p.m. was the busiest time of the day. So I drove my car back on the interstate unharmed, and screamed out loud, "LORD I cannot stand the pain!" These were outright reminders of labor pains in my belly. Having birthed three children I knew the pain well.

So when my breath seems to vanish from me, immediately God works a miracle. I breathe freely in Him. David knew for sure I that God takes care of His people, same as do I. I love and adore the way he praised God and passed it on for someone like me to share saying.

> "I will love You O LORD, my strength. The LORD is my rock my fortress and my deliverer; My God, my strength, in who I will trust; My shield and the horn of my salvation, my stronghold. I will call upon the LORD, who is worthy to be praised; so I shall be saved from my enemies," **Psalm 18:1-4**.

It happened for me that day, when my car plowed through weeds and grass in that medium. I am in awe that I am alive.

> "As for God, His way is perfect; the word of the LORD proves He is a shield to all who trust in Him," verses **30**.

I made it home safely to give my testimony. I said to God, LORD I can hear You; working two jobs was senseless and I needed to choose the one I liked best, because working one job and witnessing for Him, was enough. I quickly found out again; God's way is perfect. If we allow Him to speak to us and obey, He will direct our path safety.

> "Therefore I will give thanks to You, O LORD, among the Gentiles and sing praises to Your name Great deliverance He gives to His king, and shows mercy to His anointed To David and his descendants forevermore," verses **49-50**.

I'm thankful to be included. For out of a weeded medium, I cried out to God for help kept me safe and gave me a way to escape these things.

> "John answered and said, a man cannot receive nothing unless it has been given to Him from heaven. You yourselves bear witness that I said, I am not the Christ. But I have been sent before Him. He who has the bride-groom; but the friend of the bridegroom stands and hears him rejoices greatly, because of the bridegroom's voice." **John 3:27-29a**.

All of a sudden I recognize double blessings, and I see the words of witness.

> "Therefore this joy of mine is fulfilled. He must increase but I must decrease," **verses 29b-30;** it is truth. "He who comes from above is above all," **V 31a,** reveals His results **verses 31b-36**. "Out of darkness into His marvelous light, glimpses back reveals everyone did what was right in his own eyes," **Judges 17:6 and 21:25**.

Imagine today, if God purposely chose Ruth of the Moabites, for times like these in the midst of a battle, immigration laws, because her character shows His divine purposes and benefits. An inspired thought flashed in my spirit from the anonymous author, thanks to God. Our oldest sisters' name is Ruth, who reminds me of this renowned woman. For God loves the three of us and we love God, knowing He first loved us.

Before I continued meditating on His great plan of salvation, I am shook up within my spirit by His works in action. His Book is a famed and stunning love story that keeps me in a state of awe and fulfillment! Here three women greet each other in hurt; perfectly revealing sorrows in this life on earth.

"Looking to Jesus," I believe Paul's God breathed message for all people is to make the best of life on earth and record the facts of life in Christ.

> "To the praise of the glory of His grace, by which He made us accepted in the beloved. In Him we have redemption through His blood, the forgiveness' of sins according to the riches of His grace:" **Ephesians 1:6-7**.

Gazing at the Book of Ruth, these immigrants sound like us; God's people. We are one blood line that manifests a family affair.

> "Which He made to abound toward us in all wisdom and prudence having made known to us the mystery of His will, according to His good pleasure which he purposed in Himself, that in the dispensation of the fullness of the times He might gather together in one all things in Christ, both which are on earth in Him." **Verses 9-10**

God and His marvelous love, "looking to Jesus," **see Ruth 1:1-7,** majestically show they moved forward.

> "And Naomi said to her two daughters-in-law, Go, return each to her mother's house. The LORD deal kindly with you, as you have dealt with the dead and with me. The LORD grants that you may fine rest, each in the house of her husband; so she kissed

them, and they lifted up the voices and wept."
Verses 1:8-9

So "Jesus wept," **John 11:35**. Naomi had a time to weep. Her husband passed away along with two sons. She was broken in spirit and had no money in a foreign land, yet she released her daughters-in-laws. She said to the two of them:

> "Turn back, my daughters, go, for I am too old to have a husband: If I should say I have hope, if I should have a husband tonight and should have sons. Would you wait for them?" **Verses 12-13a**.

Ruth's plan was different from Orpah's, her assignment was to return to her hometown but both women loved Naomi.

> "Then they lifted up clung to her," **v 14**.

Amazingly it looked like Naomi was going to be alone on her way home. This amazed me.

> "But Ruth said entreat me not to leave you; or turn back from following after you: For wherever you go, I will go. And wherever you lodge I will lodge. Your people shall be my people and your God my God." **Verses 16**

These things appeared as if Ruth was licensed and bonded in His greatness to stick by Naomi like super glue.

> "When she saw that she was determined to go with her, she stopped speaking to her. Now the two of them went until they come to Bethlehem. And it happened, when they came to Bethlehem that the entire city was excited, because of them; and the women said, is this Naomi?" **Verses 18-19**

These things show to use God given sense to refuse bitterness. Even when I cry, "LORD, I cannot stand the pain," He knows when enough is enough. This is the reason the story excites me so; from the top of my head to the soles of my feet. Yet it seemed she had no mercy in her voice, saying.

> "Do not call me Naomi; call me Mara, for the Almighty has dealt very bitterly with me. I went out full, and the LORD has brought me home again empty. Why do you call me Naomi, since the LORD has testified against me, and the Almighty has afflicted me?" **Verses 20-21**

She had down time in her life, yet God does not forget His people. She changed her name to that which meant pleasant.

> "So Naomi returned, and Ruth the Moabitess her daughter-in-law with her; who returned from the country of Moab. Now they came to Bethlehem at the beginning of barley harvest," **verses 22**.

Evidently, it was the right season to return at harvest time; beyond the time of lip talk and flip flopping. It was a God thing.

> "There was a relative of Naomi's husband a man of great wealth of the family of Elimelech: His name

was Boaz: So Ruth, the Moabitess said to Naomi, Please let me go to the field glean heads of grain after him in whose sight I may fine favor: And she said Go my daughter," **2:1-2**.

In God it was all very good;

> "Then she left, and went to gleam in the field after the reapers. And she happened to come to the field belonging to Boaz, who was of the family of Elimelech." **Verse 3**

God gives us the ability to taste, touch, smell, sight, and to hear. He is absolute, especially when women of faith speak and seek pleasant company. He will work it out.

For this cause, we reap what we sow whether good or bad. As for me, I'm ready for God's great storehouse blessings that keep me humble, and show a way of escape to greater blessings in Him. Even ladies of faith have to wait on Him.

> "Now behold, Boaz came from Bethlehem and said to the reapers, The LORD be with you! And they answered him; The LORD bless you!" **Verse 4, see verses 5-7 as well.**

An elderly pastor once said, "Mothers should teach their daughters like Naomi taught Ruth, who met a wealthy faith based husband." The Book, four chapters awesomely blessed, reveals excellent choices; mindfully aware God spoke to Boaz before time.

> "Then Boaz said to Ruth, you will listen, my daughter, will you not? Do not go to glean in another field, nor go from here, but stay close to my young women," **verse 8**.

In God, it is to be continued since love, grace and mercy met in Him. And Boaz declared:

> "Let your eyes be on the field which they reap, and go after them. Have not I commanded the young men not to touch you? And when you are thirsty go to the vessels drink from what the young men have drawn." **Verse 9**.

Inspiringly, God's plan revealed love at first sight, so the bride-to-be got the message.

> "So she fell on her face, bowed down to the ground and said to him, why have I found favor in your eyes, that you should take notice of me, since I'm a foreigner? "And Boaz answered and said to her it has been fully reported to me, all that you have done for your mother-in-law since the death of your husband." **verses 10-11a**

The rich man of God reminded Ruth of her faith:

> "And how you have left your father and mother, the land of your birth, and have come to a people whom you did not know before: The LORD repay your work and a full reward to be given you by the LORD God of Israel, under whose wings you have for refuge." **Verses 11b-12**

Harvest time worked out for Ruth, a foreigner from the land of Moab. She did not look for a husband. God alone works like that. David, the sweet psalmist of Israel, made it plain. For example wrote:

"How precious is Your loving kindness, O God!
Therefore the children of men put their trust under
the shadow of Your wings," **Psalm 36:7**.

Ruth had her own request. She made it plain, in her
entering of the hall of fame.

"Then she said, let me find favor in your sight, my
lord; for you have comforted me, and spoken kindly
to your maidservant, though I'm not like your
maidservants," **Ruth 2:13**.

I believe Boaz invited Ruth to eat with him at the head
table. Its' only four chapters reread the book. But, if you
will see **verses 14-18** her mother-in-law asked a question in
verse 19 then,

"Naomi said to her daughters-in-law, blessed be he
of the LORD, who has not forsaken His kindness to
the living and the dead! And Naomi said to her this
man is a relative of ours, one of our close relatives."
Verse 20.

God reminded me of top of the mountain faith. In Him
show love for everyone; Jews and Gentiles. See Him work
all things out, **verses 21-23**. It's not my imagination,
although God has given me great imaginative ideas in
absolute abundance in Him. Ruth, my dear readers, shows
great impartiality for men and women of faith in God as a
result. By the time we sit down and revisit the book of
Ruth, who was from the country of Moab, we will know
His love, grace, and mercies met together, called the great
faith of God.

Salvation, by faith, is an act of God in the first place through His Son Jesus. A song writer got it right when he wrote: "love and marriage goes together like a horse and carriage." When I was young and in love for the first time, these things remind me of God's love, I never forgot Him. Naomi was tested, tried in sorrow yet she found a closer walk with her God, and said to Ruth.

> "Therefore wash yourself and anoint yourself, put on your best garment and go down to the threshing floor; but do not make yourself known to the man until he has finished eating and drinking. Then when he lies down, you shall go uncover his feet, and lie down; and he will tell you what you should do." **Verses 3:3-4**.

Ruth obeyed Naomi. What a God spoken blessing, in which she accepted and obeyed her mother-in-law's words of divine wisdom, I believe works through His people famously.

> "And Ruth said to her, all that you say I will do," verse 5. Yet Ruth expected her blessings; I believe her mind was made up expectantly as it is recorded saying. "Now it happened at midnight that the man was startled, and turned himself, and there was a woman lying at his feet." **Verse 8.**

I believe in her midnight hour the joy of God was her delight, for example a woman recorded a song, maybe at midnight titled. "Mama Said There Will Be Days Like This, My Mama Said."

> "So Boaz took Ruth, she became his wife and he went in to her, the LORD gave her conception, and she bore a son," **Ruth 4:13**.

Young people use noted phrases in all generations. The phrase of today, as for one in particular they say: That's what I'm talking about. Yet God's love works greater in Him every day says.

> "Then the women said to Naomi, blessed be the LORD, who has not left you this day without a close relative; and may his name be famous in Israel!" **4:14.**

Unnamed women of faith, who are God's cream of the crop, are used to prophesy His 'blessings. For instance:

> "And may he be a restorer of life and a nourisher of your old age; for your daughter-in-law, who loves you, who is better than seven sons, has born him," **verse 15**. "Then Naomi took the child and laid him on her bosom and became a nurse to him. Also the neighbor women gave him a name, saying there is a son born to Naomi. And they called his name Obed: He is the father of Jesse, the father of David, **vv 16-17.**

Imagine had Naomi been mother of seven sons, borne to her. They could not match Ruth's love to her. For the cause, one thing is clear as blue skies destine to its color by God only. Naomi's bitterness of soul showed hurt, and sorrow yet she was destined at the beginning for God to use her on purpose, He did not allow her to give up even in her down time, could've been midnight.

Years ago someone very dear to my heart, suffered a great loss of her first baby girl: years later, God opened her womb at His own time, she conceived. God blessed the two of them their son was born one Father's day morning her husband was marvelously stirred up his faith; Joy filled their home for their new born son. That remind me of a young lady who learned a song writer's hit record and song it titled I believe, "God Said It, And I Believe It, And That Settles It."

A great family affair was passed to all generation anyone may revisit verses 18-21, I copy.

> "Obed begot Jesse, and Jesse begot David." **Verse 22.**

Then I said God where do I go from here? The next day I opened my Bible in awe to 1st Samuel, God is my witness it is written saying.

> "This was a man went up from his city yearly to worship and sacrifice to the LORD of hosts in Shiloh. Also the two sons of Hophni and Phinehas, the priests of the LORD, were there. And when the time came for Elkanan to make offering, he would give potions to Peninnah his wife and to all his sons and daughters," **1st Samuel 1:3-4.**

It's an old act that works for us, never give up on God.

> "But to Hannah he would give her a double potion, for he loved Hannah, although the LORD had closed her womb. And her rival also provoked her

severely to make her miserable, because the LORD closed her womb." **Verses 5-6.**

Rethinking on the way certain people made fun of women that could not have children in those days as a child. I wondered why a family member was childless woman. Being curious I dared not ask our dear sweet mother she may have shared her opinions, on the other hand she may not have. But I remember she taught us to stay out of grown folks' businesses. So when I disobeyed her instructions all she had to say to me, was ah LORD. I got her message in the fear of God and did not get a whipping. I obeyed her words. As I grew older, I believe she may have prayed **Jeremiah 32:17**, saying, "Ah LORD! Behold You have made the heavens and the earth by Your great power and outstretched arm. There is nothing to hard for You."

Imagination is an act creating great ideas, but God's truth in not imaginary. The following words are paraphrased to natural words we use: faith in Him is unseen hope.

Hannah's name make me shame, it means grace. Had it not been for God's grace in my in my life, down time could've kept me in sorrow.

> "So it was yearly when she went up to the house of the LORD that she provoked her; therefore she wept and did not eat." 1st Samuel 1:**7**

It's a miserable act to provoke an innocence person in the house of the LORD. **See verses 8-9.** Elkanak's words to her kept me from scorners; I believe helps women of faith to hold on saying.

> "And she was in bitterness of soul, and prayed to the LORD and wept in anguish:" verses **10**.

One thing I know, our God accepts our prayers. Even in bitterness of soul, He knows us.

> "Then she made a vow and said, O LORD of hosts, if you will indeed look on my affliction of Your maidservant and remember me and not forget your maidservant, but will give Your maidservant a male child, then I will give him to the LORD all the days of his life, and no razor shall come upon his head." **Verse 11.**

Fervently in her down time, she prayed to God and her faith worked miracles saying.

> "And it happened, she continued praying before the LORD then Eli watched her mouth: Now Hannah spoke in her heart; only her lips moved, but her voice was not heard. Therefore Eli thought she was drunk. And Eli said how long will you be drunk? Put away your wine from you!" **verses 12-14.**

Eli watched only her lips move, but heard no sound, he judged her character. Same as, "A certain priest passed on the other side."

> "But Hannah answered and said my lord. I am a woman of sorrowful spirit. I have drunk neither wine nor intoxicating drink, but have poured out my soul before the LORD." **Verse 15,** See Hannah in abundance. Because she trusted her Jehovah God,

verse **16**. So then, Hannah escaped a bitter spirit with a seed of faith planted by God Almighty.

"Then Eli answered and said: Go in peace and the God of Israel grant your petition which you asked of Him." **verse 17 revealed in versed 18-19** in her due season:

"So it came to pass in the process of time that Hannah conceived and bore a son and called his name Samuel saying, for I have asked for him from the LORD." **Verses 20** see **21-26.**

We haven't seen God, but a taste of her blessing reveal she testified singing like He was there.

"For this child I prayed, and the LORD has granted me my petition which I asked of Him. Therefore I also have lent to the LORD; as long as he lives he shall be lent to the LORD. So they worshipped the LORD there," **verses 27-28**.

Samuel's name means asked of Him.

A young lady close to my heart was on her way to church one Sunday, but she knocked on my door. She was in pain, because a few weeks before, she had miscarried. God absolutely is great. That same day, God is witness; I had just reread Hannah's true story God's grace manifested awesomely. So I shared with her our LORD's blessing to Hannah. The young lady gleamed with joy in excitement, by faith in God. So it's good to see Hannah's high praise. **Chapter, 2:1-21**.

So I share a taste of her test. She talked and walked differently with an invitation to all barren women by faith in our God Almighty. I believe people of God should pray ask Him likewise.

> "Hannah prayed and said, my heart rejoices in the LORD; my horn is exalted in the LORD. I smile at my enemies, because I rejoice in Your salvation. Talk no more so very proudly; Let no arrogance come from your mouth." **2:1-3a**.

Hannah acknowledged her God on record. So women of faith by His grace, He is noticeably great and all we have to do is believe God's Word is absolute as written.

> "For the LORD is the God of knowledge; and by Him actions are weighed. The bows of the mighty men are broken, and those who stumble are girded with strength," **2: 3b-4**.

It pays to practice good speech. Then Hannah miraculously received the Word and talked about God's supernatural miracles saying:

> "The LORD makes poor and makes rich; He brings low and lifts up. He raises the poor from the dust. And lifts the bagger from the ash heap, to set them among princes: and make them inherit the throne of glory;" **verses 7-8a**.

Many young people today have a saying: it's all good! I believe the doors of the storehouses are open. I recommend wait; stand on His Word. Hannah cried out to Him likewise. She suffered in pain during her down time. God tested her faith in likeness of a cushion; a safe pillar to lay her head on. It may have been midnight or early in the dew of the morning, but she sang:

> "For the pillars of the earth are the LORD'S, and He has set the world upon them. He will guard the feet of His saints, but the wicked will be silent in darkness, for by strength no man shall prevail." Verses **8b-9**.

For example, a young lady said on T.V. told that her parents weren't rich, and if one doesn't have money, they get pushed back to the end. Yet she continues in business on T.V. I wonder how she made it to the top of the roof. **See verses 10-19**.

> "And Eli would bless Elkanan and his wife, saying: The LORD gives you descendants from the woman, for the loan that was given to the LORD. Then they would go to their own home: And the LORD visited Hannah so that she conceived and bore three sons and two daughters; meanwhile the child Samuel grew before the LORD." **Verses 20-21**.

Preciously, I offer praise to God in Christ throughout my book. For example, being seventy-one years old, a woman of faith in God, happy or sad, I speak out, LORD where do I go from here? It works! Glancing over my life as a young woman, I was interviewed for two good jobs, but was denied both positions, because I wore a curly afro. Very popular in those days, I thought I looked pretty nice.

They said character-wise my attitude was fine, but I had to change my hair style. As a young mother of two little girls, extra money was not in our budget. This was the main reason I had to work. As a result, I walked home very sad. I thought in wonder, because a white lady clerk at their bank recommended me, plus I had opened a checking account at the bank which is in business today. A dollar store, still open today, needed a clerk. I did not get hired there either, but they accepted my money all of these many years; so be it. May God bless America!

This brings to mind an interview on cable news with a seven year old little black girl, who was told by her school that her hairstyle was unacceptable. The journalist talked with both the little girl and her father who both showed good character. In the end, teachers voted in favor of the little girl.

I continue to pray fervent, wonder working prayers that cause me to stick to God's blessings. Yet if I should write my true story, the pain, hurt, sorrow and shame is apt to distract my attention. But one thing I know one. My second God breathed book will manifest my abundant joy, and will reveal the divine struggles He has allowed to test me.

In likeness, the anonymous psalmist summarized Hannah's test, with her name attacked, but God. It is an excellent task to pray on saying what I know is true.

> "He grants the barren woman a home like a joyful mother of children: Praise the LORD," **Psalm 113:9**.

The Apostle Paul wrote,

> "First I thank God through Jesus Christ for you all, that your faith is spoken of throughout the world. God is my witness whom I serve in my spirit in the gospel of His Son that without ceasing I make mentions of you always in my prayers." **Romans 1:8-10**.

These things reveal thanksgiving to God and I offer thanks alike seen within verses 11-15. As a result, Paul says:

> "For I am not ashamed to preach the gospel of Christ, for it is the power of God to salvation for everyone who believes, for the Jew first and also to the Greek. For in it the righteousness of God revealed from faith to faith; as it is written, the just shall live by faith." **Verses 16-17**

Jew or Greek it takes faith. God is witness and I second the motion for actions moving forward in Him. Then the writer revealed questions and answers. In the process, believers and unbelievers are welcome to follow:

> "For which of the angels did He ever say: You are My Son, and again: I will be to Him a Father: And He shall be to Me a Son? But when He brings the first born into the world, He says: Let all the angels of God worship Him. And of the angels He says:

Who makes His angels' spirits and His ministers a flame of fire." **Hebrews 1:5-7**.

I express in writings again;

"But to the Son He says Your throne, O God, is forever and ever: a scepter of righteousness is the scepter of Your kingdom. You have loved righteousness and hated lawlessness; therefore God, Your God, has anointed You with the oil of gladness more that Your companion." **Verses 8-9**

God is infinite Royalty. A scepter is a baton of royalty. It manifests Esther's love to her king and he adored her.

"She had neither father nor mother; the young lady was of great beauty when her mother and father died Mordecai took her as his own daughter." **Esther 2:7b**.

The king loved the lady of royalty big time.

"So when the king saw Queen Esther standing in the court that she found favor in his sight, the king held out to Esther the golden scepter that was in his hand. Then Esther went near and touched the top of the scepter." Chapter **5:2**

So I greet **Wonder**'s best ever, in my God given book. Great blessings call my attention to **Wonder** many times; I wonder how we made it. A writer penned, "It Is Jesus." They say **Wonder** had the best marching band ever.

One day I met a former student of Wonder High in a marketplace. We were in the check-out line when he called my name. He told me he was attending a thirty-year class reunion in honor to **Wonder**. Then he remembered I was leader of the majorettes. He told me his name which was easy to remember, since he had the same name as my first grandson. He was celebrating their thirtieth year reunion. I was speechless. We were celebrating fifty-one years at **Wonder**!

Glancing back, God promoted us from New St Paul church and made room for us. Our books were provided by the white school. Whereas they, the white folk, received new books, we used their old ones along with their hand-me-down type-writers, desks, etc. We had to pay for typing classes, unlike children today, and complaints didn't help us since: "The common people heard Him gladly." **Mark 12:37b**.

"They" say we performed excellent on 8th and Broadway. That is whoever desired to watch us swirl our batons. The truth makes happy faces of majorettes of **Wonder High** rejoice in our golden years in excellence. So I greet each of us in my own book. Those of us who remain alive today, hopefully will read these things and celebrate the purified truth.

I have sweet memories of **Wonder**'s former principal who taught us; former teachers, musicians and trainers of **Wonder**; and of the many former students who graduated and prepared for colleges. Also I greet the former cheerleader, and great cooks in food service hall of the fame, who our dear mother was a part of. And to our grandfather who labored in maintenance. Thanks to God, El-ee-Shaw who hears us; Home of the **Wonder** Lions.

So then, Paul got it right. He left his mark and I share his great greetings.

> "Grace to you and peace from God our Father and the LORD Jesus Christ: Blessed be the God and Father of our LORD Jesus Christ, who has blessed us with every spiritual blessing in heavenly places in Christ." **Ephesians 1:2-3**.

His immeasurable blessings manifest "the sons of Korah," I believe a family affair:

> "Mercy and truth have met together righteousness and peace has kissed: Truth shall spring out of the earth: And righteousness shall look down from heaven. Yes, the LORD will give what is good, and our land will yield its increase. Righteousness will go before Him and shall make His footsteps our pathway." **Psalm 85:10-13; see verses 1-9**.

And I greet expert former trumpet players, drummers and saxophonists. Likewise, my youngest grandson practices saxophone in the midst of an expert.

One of my former **Wonder** classmates helped her twin grandsons enter college in a big time city. They tried out for the band, with both chosen to perform in, I believe, 'The Battle of the Drums', and the two graduated from that college in 2012. As I do believe they continued in their music with an expert passion. God's blessings are family affairs. Wonder High School's best, with our great golden years to be loved by God in abundance so be it.

Chapter Two
"Within and Outward"

> "Behold, how good and how precious it is for
> brethren to dwell together in unity! It is like
> precious oil upon the head running down on the
> beard of Aaron, running down on the edge of his
> garments." **Psalm 133:1-2**.

Preciously, in memory of my dear husband, I chose praise
blessings to reveal his eulogy in full, for:

> "It is like the dew of Herman, descending upon the
> mountain of Zion: For there the LORD commanded
> the blessing of life for evermore." **Verses 3**.

My heart's desires remain. God said stick to His blessings,
Amen.

A song writer penned a song titled, "It is like the Dew of
Heaven." A young lady in the choir, sang it as if she wrote
it.

But Moses wrote:

> "The LORD bless and keep you; the LORD make
> his face to shine upon you; And be gracious to you,
> the LORD lift up His countenance upon you and
> give you peace." **Numbers 6:24-26**.

Another writer wrote a well known song, "We fall Down
but We Get Up." When words are spoken out loud, He
hears us; even in our thoughts; the God of all hearing, El-
Shaddy Almighty. The unnamed psalmist asked a question
and answered:

> "How shall we escape if we neglect so great a salvation, which at the first began to be spoken by the LORD, and was confirmed to us by those who heard Him, God also bearing both with signs and wonders with various miracles, and gifts of the Holy Spirit, according to His own will?" **Hebrews 2:3-4**.

By faith it is written:

> "But we see Jesus, who was made a little lower than the angels, for the sufferings of death, crowned with glory and honor and He by the grace of God might taste death for everyone." **Verse 9, see verses 10-15**.

One thing is reality. Jesus is really God's daily grace. For instance, I sat down and listened to the evidence of a young man very close to my heart, telling of his struggles and hard times. He said a pastor helped him with unseen hope. Then to make it plain to me spiritually, he used his finger to make his point. He pointed four ways: east, west, north and south, as if he plucked four invisible angels in favor of Jesus Christ, who is our unseen hope. I was inspired beyond vocabulary to express vocally, or in writing, its perfection fitting His greatness. For example: Our shoe size, whether saved or unsaved, reminds me that in Him, one size fits all; yet it is by faith in God that there is a choice to believe in His unseen hope.

Quickened by the Holy Spirit, I'm reminded what great things Jesus said, things that hold my complete attention during my down time. And it works when we stay focused. He said:

"Verily, verily, I say unto you, He that enters not by the door into the sheepfold, but climbs up some other way, the same is a thief and a robber: But he that enters in by the door is the shepherd of the sheep. To him the potter opened; and the sheep hear His voice and he calls His own sheep by name. And lead them out." **John 10:1-3**.

Jesus is Instructor, the Good Shepherd:

"And when he puts forth His own sheep, He goes before them and the sheep follow Him, for they know His voice**." Verses 4-5**

So it is a good thing that captures my thoughts, because we walked and talked these things in the streets of our hometown making it known to many.

"A stranger will they not follow, but will flee from him: for they know not the voice of strangers." **Verse 5 see verses 6-9**, for "The thief comes not, but for to steal and to kill and to destroy: I Am come, that they might have life and that they may have it more abundantly:" **verse 10**.

He promised us more than enough, He who illustrated in likeness of a picture or hand print on the wall of hands folded together in prayer. God our promise keeper He said.

"And I give unto them eternal life, and they shall never perish; neither shall any man pluck them out of My hand. My Father, who has given them to Me, is greater than all; and no man is able to pluck them out of My Father's hand. I and My Father are one.

Then the Jews picked up stones again to stone Him." **Verse 29-30**

See Jesus and His questions manifested in **verses 32, 34** and **36**. The end verse tells it like it is:

"And then many believed on Him there." **Verse 42**

An elderly deacon opened devotion faithfully on Sunday morning singing, "I Will Trust In The LORD Till I Die." He wasn't a lead singer, but he sang as if he were. He stuck to the greatest things he knew, in singing, "Walk with Me LORD, Walk with Me."

Purposely, the amazing psalmist continued with the testimony of the righteousness of God.

"For indeed He does not give aid to angels, but He does give aid to the seed of Abraham." **Hebrews 2:16**.

God rewarded our deacon with a new wife who bore him a baby girl in his elder years. She was their first baby together. The two also raised an adopted daughter before he passed away years later. He was loved and respected by many. Later his dear wife died. But before she passed, she and her mom sang together, "Give Her the Flowers While She Lives." In sweet memories, they had down times on earth, but trusted God who walked with them daily.

Nahum declared:

"The LORD is good a stronghold in the day of trouble; And He knows those who trust in Him." **Nahum 1:7**.

It is very good for us to express our love to Him indeed. Yet when I find it too hard to say vocally or record what is on my mind, I think on David's record which works perfectly as it is written.

> "O LORD, our LORD, How excellent is Your name in all the earth, Who have set Your glory above the heavens! Out of the mouth of babes and nursing infants: You have ordained strength, because of Your enemies, That You may silence, the enemy and the avenger. When I consider Your heavens, the work of Your fingers" **Psalm 8:1-3a**.

A young lady sang a song as if she practiced the words while gazing up at,

> "The moon and the stars which You have ordained, What is man that You are mindful of him, and the son of man that You visited him?" **Verse 3b-4**

Then it happened. One cool Sunday morning, while we were searching for a good place to eat breakfast in a big city, my fourteen year old granddaughter, spotted a poor man lying on a nearby rooftop fast asleep. She remarked to her younger siblings that at least the poor man could lie in the sun to keep warm. For me this was remarkable. To my surprise, I realized my granddaughter had compassion, which made me smile.

In a place with a few people in number, a lady revealed to then Senator Obama a lesson she learned. She the shouted, "I'm fired up and ready to go!" After that, *I* was fired up with joy. A chief musician skillfully described God's handmade man:

> "For You have made him a little lower that the angels and You have crowned him with glory and honor. You made him to have dominion over the works of Your hands; You have put all things under his feet, all sheep and oxen; Even the beast of the field;" **verse 5-7**.

God promoted him in quiet pastures. I believe four legged animals were included in likeness and,

> "The birds of the air and the fish of the sea that pass through the paths of the seas: O LORD, our LORD How excellent is Your name in all the earth."
> **Verses 8-9**

My dear readers, any one of us, during our down time, could allow distractions to separate us from our God given joy, of our LORD and Savior Jesus Christ. Remember Job gave an example of how love worked, when he talked about the great sea beast leviathan. He described God's love to us in action, as he revealed the beast to encourage us.

> "His rows of scales are his pride shut us tight as a seal: One is so close that no air can come between them. They are joined one to another; they stick together cannot be parted" **Job 41:15-17**.

For example, Democrats work together in hope we cannot see. It's a pleasure to see them working to let all nations know we the people are united. Whosoever is invited to pass on love has many splendid colors. Jesus said:

> "And you shall know the truth, and the truth will make you free," **John 8:32**. So "Then Job answered the LORD and said: I know You can do

everything and no purpose of Yours can be withheld from you. And You asked who is this who hides council without knowledge? Therefore I have uttered what I did not understand things to wonderful for me that I did not know." Job **42:1-3**.

In abundance I write blessings stored in my God given memory and I love to say God is my witness. One day at noon, facing north praying, while bowed on my knees, God said to vote in the Primary for Obama. I was greatly stunned. I had never voted before time. I leapt to my feet and called my oldest daughter born who was born the same year as Obama and shared what God said. Her response was, "mama I know you are right He said we do not support our men enough." My youngest daughter also believed, but my son said, "we will see mama." Awe inspired, I casted my vote. These things caused me to adore God more abundantly. Paul said:

> "I planted, Apollos watered, but God gave the increase:" **1st Corinthians 3:6**

Many people were lined up to vote inward and outwardly; a wondrous sight to see. We waited in long lines, excited to cast a vote for our first black President. Being the son of a black father and white mother was no accident. And let me tell you. The power of God was in that place, my dear readers. Job said:

> "Listen, please and let me speak: You said I will question you, and you shall answer Me. I have heard of You by the hearing of the ear, now my eyes see You. Therefore I abhor myself and repent

in dust and ashes. So it was, after the LORD has spoken." **Job 42: 4-6; see verses 7-9**

So we know the true glory story works:

"And the LORD restored Job's losses when he prayed for his friends. Indeed the LORD gave Job twice as much as he had before." **Verse 10**.

In fact, in God, the last verses are recorded based on destiny. From the beginning in Him is greatly revealed **see verses 10b-17**. Therefore, the President and Vice President need our prayers day and night privately and publicly; likened unto an angel carrying a message or as John, the forerunner of Jesus, son of Elizabeth and Zacharias. Yes we can! **See and revisit Luke 1:13-14.**

God awesomely used an angel to bring news when the children of Israel did evil. God always had a ram on earth. For example:

"Manoah, his wife was barren had no children," **Judges 13**.

Their son Samson was born to be judge of Israel twenty years. What's age or being barren got to do with God's marvelous works and acts? Absolutely nothing! For years ago, He reminded me to revisit **Psalms 23** every day of my life, and I just do it.

Months later proved President Obama was no racist nor did he specialize in racism. He campaigned in a place that said just vote don't boo. I was excited to hear him speak God given wisdom from above. It paid off favorably for him and me also. Because four days before Election Day God conspicuously forewarned me in my kitchen that Senator Obama would be the 44th President of the United States of America. Clearly, I believed Him. I cannot explain God's greatness, but in Him Paul said:

> "And we know that all things work together for good to those who love God, to those who are the called according to His purpose." **Romans 8:28**

And I greatly love God inside and out! Yet I try to describe the results in my writings that still remain indescribably.

I telephoned everyone; family; friends; extended family, and witnessed to them the greatest news report, as only God can do for someone like me, in the hours spent rereading, meditating and diligently seeking Him every day of my life. My son was my first call. He said, mama, "God did reveal the President of the United States of America to you." And I thank God always, for He provides a witness to affirm His Word. Then I watched President Obama and Vice President Biden run in circles together on T.V. and likewise I leapt up and ran in circles in my house with my telephone ringing all night long. I could barely wait for Sunday morning services to reiterate my wide awake vision. Yet by grace I made it and testified in the midst of my pastor at time of thirty-five years and members excitedly blessed in God to pass it on.

Earlier, my former pastor said Senator Clinton was apt to win the race to the White House. He was not the only pastor who spoke their beliefs which was fine with me, so be it. I stuck to my vision in the midst of those seated within service. Paul wrote:

> "I thank my God upon every remembrance of your. Always in every prayer of mine making request for you all with joy, for the fellowship in the gospel from the first day until now." **Philippians 1:2-5**.

Honestly, I pray fervently day and night that God bless our president and vice president beyond their knowledge, because it is the right thing to do for our country's leaders.

Paul recorded instructions to remain focused and balanced in God. So I copy his record. As for me,

> "Being confident of this very thing, that He who begun a good work in you will complete it until the day of Jesus Christ." **Verse 6**.

Struggling, striving, singing, praying, praising and lifting up the name of Jesus is life. God works beyond talk that is easy, but my writings are entirely different as day and night on earth. My assignment keeps me stroking with the words, "Be of good courage." Words hang on my door year round encourage me.

> "Rejoice in the LORD always, again, I say Rejoice. Let your moderations be known to all men. The LORD is at hand. Be careful for nothing; but in everything by prayer and supplication with thanksgiving let your request be known to God." **Philippians 4:4-6**.

It is a very good thing when God speaks. My duty is to listen attentively and be willing to obey Him.

> "And, the peace of God which passes all
> understanding shall keep your hearts and minds
> through Jesus Christ." **Verse 7**.

So it's great praying for peace on earth since, President
Obama and Vice President Biden days, I believe, in the
White House are peace makers indeed. Therefore, between
the two of them, they constantly talk of peace on earth,
good will to all people. I believe the two are doing great
and mighty works; yet the words that stay on my door and
stick in my heart says:

> "Finally, brethren, whatever things are true,
> whatever things are honest, whatever things are just,
> whatever things are pure, whatever things are
> lovely, whatever things are of good report, if there
> be any virtue and if there be any praise, think on
> these things" **Verse 8**.

Finally, character-wise, Paul selected by God wrote a way
for us to get right and stay rich. It's gainful, in that God's
blessings are with Mr. Obama, with his wife, our first Lady
Mrs. Michelle Obama, and their two adorable daughters.
Likewise, I offer God's blessings to Mr. Biden along with
his wife, Dr. Jill Biden; all who are people of faith aim to
help others that will believe.

Paul added:

> "But I rejoiced in the LORD greatly that now at the
> last your care for me has flourished again." **v 10a**;
> Paul said, "I can do all things through Christ who
> strengthens me." **Verse 13**

So then, we know leaders of the free world need our infinite prayers, because we serve an infinite God, although we are finite. He said:

> "Nevertheless you have done well that you share in my distress" **v 14**. Great news reveals the purified truth, as it is written. "And my God shall supply all your needs according to His riches in glory by Christ Jesus. Now to our God and Father be glory forever and ever" **verses 19-20**. The true glory story ends with key note blessings in Him says: "The grace of our LORD Jesus Christ be with you all. Amen." **Verse 23**

Anonymously a psalmist recorded an invitation I call a winner's hit saying on purpose.

> "Make a joyful shout to the LORD, all you lands! Serve the LORD with gladness; Come before His presence with singing. Know that the LORD, He is God; it is He that made us and not ourselves; we are His people and the sheep of His pasture." **100:1-3**.

Today the invitation remains open to,

> "Enter into the gate with thanksgiving, and into His courts with praise. Be thankful to Him and bless His name: For the LORD is good His mercy is everlasting and His truth endures to all generations." **Verses 4-5**

God sent His Word for His people to imitate Him joyfully. David accepted the offer and said:

> "I was glad when they said to me let us go into the house of the LORD. Our feet have been standing

within your gates, O Jerusalem. Jerusalem is built as a city compact together; Where the tribes go up; the tribes of the LORD, To the Testimony of Israel, to give thanks to the name of the LORD;" **Psalms 122:1-4**.

Thanks to God, it is known in that we should,

"Pray for the peace of Jerusalem. May they prosper who love you: Peace within your walls: Prosperity within your palaces; For the sake of my brethren and companions; I will now say, Peace be within you. Because, of the house of the LORD our God; I will seek your good:" **Verses 6-9**.

I'm mindful of how we pray for peace in our homes and churches "Looking to Jesus", today we have many leaders, thanks to God.

"Unless the LORD builds the house, they labor in vain who built it; unless the LORD guards the city, the watchman stays awake in vain, it is vain for you to rise up early, to sit up late, to eat the bread of sorrows; For He gives His beloved sleep. Behold children are a heritage from the LORD, the fruit of the womb is a reward." **127:1-3**.

Solomon glorified God in likeness of July 4th fireworks that light up the sky, such as His glory fills and lights up the earth.

"Like arrows in the hand of a worrier, so are the children of one's youth. Happy is the man who has his quiver full of them; they shall not be ashamed,

but shall speak with their enemies in the gate."
Verses 4-5

Solomon regarded welfare for little children written two ways in this place.

> "A good man leaves an inheritance to his children's children, but the wealth of the sinner is stored up for the righteous." **Proverbs 13:22;** see verses **23-25.**

This is far reaching. For our elders never mention the great blessings Solomon had in mind, such as wine or cash funds. For example:

> "A feast is made for laughter and wine makes merry: But money answers everything."
> **Ecclesiastes 10:19.**

David, Solomon's father had majestic questions and answers we should know. He majestically revealed:

> "The heavens declare the glory of God and the firmament shows His handiworks. Day unto day utters speech, and night unto night reveals knowledge. There is no speech nor language where there voice is not heard. There line has gone through all the earth and their words to the end of the world:" **Psalm 19:1-4a.**

Likewise as for God:

> "He has set up a tabernacle for the sun, which is like a bridegroom coming out of his chamber; and rejoices like a strong man to run its race."
> **Verses 4b-5**:

A song writer penned "We come a Long Way, LORD a Mighty Long Way."

There was an elderly lady I picked up on Sundays, unless hindered by whatever reasons. We attended church together, before she moved to Chicago to live with her dear sister. Years before she moved, she handed me a copy of *Our Daily Bread.* I have received this booklet, at my request, for forty years and voluntarily pass on copies today. I was amazed to find a photo of Wintley Phipps, a young black man, on the cover page the March 2013 copy. God be the glory! I had a nudging within my spirit to write daily scriptures with comments likened unto O.D.B., for it's all about our God in the first place. It is recorded here for us to know:

> "Its rising is from one end of heaven and its circuit to the other end; and it is nothing hidden from the heat. The law of the LORD is perfect converting the soul. The testimony of the LORD is sure making wise the simple;" **Verses 6-7**.

The elderly lady and I exchanged letters until her dear hands were no longer able to use her pen.   In memory of her, she passed away in that big city of Chicago after many years living with her sister. She was old enough to be my mother. She loved God amazingly testified of His greatness.

> "The statues of the LORD are right rejoicing the heart; the commandment of the LORD is pure, enlightening the eyes;" **Verse 8**.

A dear friend of ours, who attended **Wonder**, grew up and had children of his own. When he visited us, he always teased our three children wondrously with: O what great big eyes you have my dear, better to see with my dear. O what great ears you have for better to hear with my dear, etc. His words truly confirmed God's blessings.

> "The fear of the LORD is clean, enduring forever; the judgment of the LORD are true and righteous altogether" v 9. His works endues forever, as it is reported to us greatly. "More to be desired are they than pure gold, yea than much fine gold, Sweeter also than honey and the honeycomb: Moreover by them Your servants are warned, and keeping in them is great reward: Who can understand his errors? Cleanse me from secret faults." **Verses 10-13** God tests our motives whether right or wrong. David requested:

> "Keep back Your servants also from presumptuous sins; Let them not have dominion over me: Then I shall be blameless: And I shall be innocent of great transgression." **Verses 13**.

Then David described four ways to practice blamelessness before God, regardless of where we live, work, or worship, he recorded:

> "Let the words of my mouth, and the mediation of my heart, be acceptable in Your sight, O LORD, my strength and my Redeemer." **Verse 14**.

Early one Sunday morning, my pastor said the Holy Spirit revealed to him that I should deliver the message. I obediently stood up, and these words flowed from my mouth:

Above was God's plan to the core of my soul. For in Him it was not imaginary; because God's words are stored in a good place within my heart and soul; blameless before Him. Because, it's my personal pray request, mostly in private, in the presence of Jesus. A praise song entered my spirit titled: "Just a Closer Walk with Thee." A writer famously wrote a hit record, whosoever may sing: "Please Be Patient with Me, God Is Not Through with Me Yet." James, the half brother of Jesus tested positive character-wise. As an expert, he recorded two choices positively. Yet I do warn us, my dear readers, it is tight, but it is right.

> "My brethren, count it all joy when you fall in various trials, knowing you faith produces patience. But let patience have its perfect work, that you may be perfect and complete, lacking nothing. If any of you lacks wisdom, let him ask of God, who gives to all men liberally and without reproach, and it shall be given to him." **James 1:2-5**.

Saving faith reveals the situation. James revealed the pathway to wisdom from above continuously saying,

> "But let him ask in faith with no doubting, for he who doubt is like a wave of the sea driven and tossed by the wind. For let not that man, suppose that he will suppose that he will receive anything from the LORD; he is a double-minded man: Unstable in all his ways." **Verses 6-8**

To be honest, two paths way are actually explained to us:

> "Let the lower brother glory in his exaltation, but the rich in his humiliation, because as a flower of the field he will pass away. For no sooner has the sun risen with a burning heat then it withers the grass; its flower fails and its beautiful appearance perishes. So the rich man will also fade away in his pursuits:" **Verses 9-11**.

Is approved because,

> "Blessed is the man who endures temptation; for when he has been approved, he will received the crowd of life which the LORD has promised to those who love Him." **Verse12**.

As results it is your thing, but James influenced by the Spirit says,

> "Let no man say when he is tempted, I am tempted by God, for God cannot be tempted by evil, nor does He Himself tempt anyone." **Verse 13** it is revealed in **verses 14-16**.

Great things we should revisit since,

> "Every good gift and every perfect gift is from above and comes down from the Father of lights with whom there is no variation or shadow of turning: Of His own will brought us forth the word of truth we might be a kind of first fruits of His creatures" **Verses 17-18**.

James absolutely reveals Jesus' followers, for his sayings are purified truth.

"So then, my beloved brethren, let every man be swift to hear, slow to speak, slow to wrath: for the wrath of man does not produce, the righteousness of God. Therefore lay aside all filthiness and overflow of wickedness's and receive with meekness, the implanted word, which is able to save your souls" verses **19-20**.

The Word carries me through mighty revelations marked, signed, sealed and delivered. Jesus is the reason I sing hooray for Good Friday. No wonder a certain Bishop chosen by God used a wonderful song, "Signed Sealed, And Delivered" whosoever believes He is Savior remains a wonder.

Mr. Obama is President. So I reiterate great things. Jesus revealing to His own disciples two path ways said:

"With men this is impossible, but with God all things are possible," Matthew 19:26; glance up: "Then Jesus said, and again I say to you, it is easier for a rich man to go through the eye of a needle than for a rich man to enter the kingdom of God." **Verse 24**.

Jesus explained the evidence two ways:

"But many who are first will be last and the last first," **verse 30**.

For example, an actor played a father's part in a movie; his younger daughter played a prodigal daughter in likeness of the prodigal son. Her father said, go and find your shoes and when you find them, ware them. Read the greatest salvation plan on earth. A way to escape jealousy; One of a kind, manifested in **Luke 15:11-32**.

James actually "stirred up the gift" with two way actions recorded.

> "But be doers of the word and not hearers only, deceiving yourselves: For if anyone is a hearer of the word and not a doer, he is like a man observing his natural face in a mirror; for he observes himself, goes away, and immediately forgets what kind of man he was;" **James 1:22-24**.

These blessings humanize believers and unbelievers, because in reality,

> "Pure and undefiled religion before God and the Father is this: to visit orphans and widows in their trouble and to keep oneself unspotted from the world." verse **27**

I said to myself, no wonder James' book is a clue to the *New Testament* book of *Proverbs*. Good verses bad, my dear readers, is revealed today and forever.

> "You pay attention to the one wearing the fine clothes say to him, you sit here in a good place, and say to the poor man, you stand there, or sit here at my footstool, have you not shown partiality among yourselves, and become judges with evil thoughts," **James 2:3-4**.

One Sunday a young lady tried to enter the sanctuary for worship service when an usher closed the door in her face. But the young lady pushed her aside and entered within. Then it happened. The look in her face revealed her attitude favored partiality as it is written. James said:

"Listen, my beloved brethren: Has God not chosen the poor of the world to be rich in faith and heirs of the kingdom that He promised to those who love Him. But you have dishonored the poor man. Do not the rich oppress you drag you into courts?" **James 2: 5-6.**

Questions in motion; yea or nay remains,

"If you really fulfill the royal law according to the Scriptures, you shall love your neighbor as yourself, you do well; but it you show partiality you commit sin, and are convicted by the law as transgressors: For whosoever shall keep the whole law and yet stumble in one point he is guilty of all." **Verses 8-10.**

I ask God to recheck my own thoughts daily. He does these things abundantly well. For one day, while on my knees, amazingly I opened my mouth and a writer's song stirred me up.

"Lead me Guide Me O Great Jehovah:" "For judgment is without mercy to the one who has shown no mercy: Mercy triumphs over judgment." **Verse 13** reread also **14-22** to show: "Faith without works is dead. "And the Scripture was fulfilled which says Abraham believed God it was accounted to him for righteousness. And he was called a friend of God justified by works and not by faith only." **Verses 23-24.**

Fortunately, James humanized a woman's fortune:

"Likewise was not Rahab, the harlot also justified by works when she received messengers and sent them out another way? For as the body without the spirit is dead, so faith without works is dead also" **Verses 25-26.**

Today a measure of red thread hangs on my bathroom window blinds. Indeed, an excellent reminder of God's immeasurable works and acts: for He approved Rahab's work of faith, because God hid her misery graciously in the Book of life. As for me, God uses whosoever, or whatever means accordingly.

> "But Joshua has said to the two men who had spied out the country, go into the harlot's house, and from there bring out the woman and all that she has as you swore to her. And the young men who had been spies went in and brought out Rahab, her father and mother, her brothers, and all her relatives and left them outside the camp of Israel:" **Joshua 6:22-23.**

An abundant family affair; her name is written within Jesus' genealogy; **Matthew 1:5**. She knew her shoe size. And James described:

> "Now the fruit of righteousness is sown in peace by those who make peace;" **James 3:18**. Amen.

Peace is without war in likeness of a billion dollar question.

> "Where do wars and fights come from among you? Do they not come from your desires for pleasure that wars in your members?" **4:1.**

Therefore what is pride in the sight of God constantly?

> "Or do you think that the Scripture says in vain;
> The Spirit who dwells in us yearns jealously?
> **Verses 5**.

Whereas jealously works worst than poison ivy, but He reveals a way to escape envy; God's way, as it is written below.

> "Therefore submit to God: Resist the devil and he will flee from you. Draw near to God and He will draw near to you. Cleanse your hands you sinners and purify your hearts you double minded. Lament and mourn and weep: Let your laughter be turned to mourning and your joy to gloom:" **4:7-9**.

Therefore he made it plain and taught us to,

> "Humble yourselves in the sight of the LORD, and He will lift you up." **10; see verses 11-16**
> "Therefore, to him who knows to do good, and does not do it, to him is sin." **V 17.**

A Good Samaritan helped made him wealthy an invitation James says,

> "Come now, you rich, weep and howl for your miseries that are coming upon you. Your riches are corrupted and your garments are moth-eaten. Your gold as silver is corroded and corrosion will be a witness against you and will eat your flesh like fire. You have heaped up treasure in the last days." **5:1-3.**

A friend of mine compares James' words to Pigford vs. Glickman; 1 and 2 class action lawsuit saying,

> "Indeed the wages of the laborers who mowed your fields that you kept back by fraud, cry out; the reapers have reaped the ears of the LORD of Sabaoth. You have lived on the earth in pleasure and luxury; you have fattened your hearts as in the days of slaughter" **Verses 4-5**.

James revealed great things to warn the rich with instructions written in his book, reveals:

> "You have condemned, you have murdered the just; he does not resist you. Therefore be patient, brethren, until the coming of the LORD: See how the farmer waits for the precious fruits of the earth, waiting patiently, for it receives the early and latter rain" **Verses 6-7**.

Years ago my Sunday school teacher asked the class to define patient. I obeyed her and turned in my work. In Greek, reveals mak-roth-oo-meh-o, in that is long-spirited, forbearing patience willing to wait, endure, long-tempered suffer-long. A former classmate of said to me, you have the patience of Job. I responded, God said there was none like Job. Praise the LORD of glory I copy a glimpse.

> "Then the LORD said to Satan have you considered My servant Job there is none like him in the earth, a perfect and upright man one that fears God, and shuns evil? And still he holds fast to his integrity, although you incited Me against him, to destroy him without cause" **Job 2:3**.

Satan challenged God and he failed; **verses 4-10.** James asked billion dollar questions.

> "Is anyone among you suffering? Let him pray. Is anyone cheerful? Let him sing psalms. Is any among you sick? Let him call for the elders, anointing him with oil in the name of the LORD" **James 5:13-14**.

A father talks to his family with purposed a way to escape war, and renew peace and wealth within his own house. He acknowledged:

> "Confess your faults one to another that you may be healed: The effective fervent prayer of a righteous man avails much" verse 16. "Let him know that he who turns a sinner from the error of his way saves a soul from death and cover a multitude of sins" **Verse 20**.

***

Greetings, black farmers, heirs and attempted farmers. It is a pleasure to make mention of us in my book. As faithful filers in regards to civil rights class action law suit, based on years of discrimination; Pigford vs. Glickman, racial discrimination against the second largest branch of government of the United States, the Department of Agriculture, against black farmers, heirs, and attempted farmers, etc. The question Habakkuk asked God, and I recall his famous question.

"The burden which the prophet Habakkuk saw,"
chapter 1:1 saying: "O LORD, how long shall I
cry and You not hear? Even cry out to You,
violence! And You will not save. Why do You
show me iniquity, And cause me to see trouble?"
verses **2-3a**

For the cause, God will answer, but we have different
strokes and tests, so Habakkuk was a bold prophet for Him.
He examined the situation and wrote the evidence saying:

"For plundering and violence are before me; there
is strife, and contention arises," **verse 3b**.

Habakkuk responded to God:

"I will stand my watch and set myself on the
rampart and watch to see what He will say to me:
And what will answer when I am corrected." **2:1**

It is a very rich and wealthy lesson he said:

"Then the LORD answered me and said: Write the
vision and make it plain on tablets; that he may run
who reads it. For the vision is yet for an appointed
time; but at the end it will speak, and not lie.
Though it tarries, wait for it; because it will surely
come, it will not tarry." **Verse 2**.

God is my witness; I've written tablets upon tablets. I'm
not tied yet; over twenty filled to the brim by faith in Him.
I write the truth to the best of my knowledge, same as did
Habakkuk recorded.

"Behold the proud, his soul is not upright in him;
But the just shall live by faith;" **verse 4**.

He embraced God's Word by faith. Many of us met years in many places in the pursuit of the plight of black farmers and those associated with them, filed affidavits too late to get paid. Those of us who sought to borrow low rate interest loans to purchases land to farm, daycare sites that serve food, etc., were denied a right to borrow as did white farmers applied and received USDA funds. I believe, under Fair Housing Act of 1949 Farmers Home Administration, or such files housed in county courthouses, were misinformed. Then we met BFAA president with lawyers; attended all meeting in pursuit of information.

Unfortunately, many pay membership fees today. But far as I know, they say their dues are for travel expenses, etc. As citizens of the United States, according to the Constitution Amendment 14th, the case is worthy to debate with congress again, because we were denied fair and just opportunities, based on racial discrimination. Then BFAA president, our lawyer, mayors, and pastors, called themselves Levites, along with a state representative, made it possible to reopened Pigford 1, traveled to Washington D.C., one day before the five year statute of limitations expired.

I believe, as God would have it, Pigford 1 was reopened to Pigford 2. So when all the above men and women returned to their hometowns, BFAA president had a call meeting at a certain place.

As volunteers, many of us spread the word; past on petitions in our hometown; and mailed many out of town. We informed people to get set to voluntarily travel to Washington D.C. The first time, bus loads of all who were involved, paid in advanced for the trip and met together from Arkansas, Tennessee and Mississippi. We traveled with BFAA president and the lawyer we retained met us there to debate our case, along with four Congressmen; two Democrats; two Republicans who introduced themselves and states they represented.

Although our agreements and affidavits were notarized, signed and returned to the lawyer, by registered mail, we thought everything was approved. But, according to the Dear John letters we received, our files never reached Portland Oregon's administrative offices.

In that, were denied our civil rights as hardworking American citizens. A congressman from Arkansas said to our faces, we had been discriminated against over one-hundred twenty years. I remember all four congressmen by name who said thousands were not paid, because racial discrimination continues. One Congressman said it would take an act of congress to pay us; an act was approved by congress, but we have not been paid, nor given up hope today.

So the second time, more bus loads journeyed to Washington. We marched behind two men in a wagon hitched to two mules, representing forty acres and a mule. We sang in the rain, 'No Justice, No Peace'. James understood politics, because Jesus owns the true government; **James 2:5**.

To my amazement, a Republican congressman invited us to Cincinnati Ohio, to inform us in the state he represented regarding Pigford 1 and 2. We accepted his invitation; paid our own expenses again, and was exceedingly glad to visit the Underground Rail Road as good Samaritans.

I'm not surprise, but we heard of a black lady, who filed a petition for farmers' relief in 1918. In fact, relief should have started back then, but she failed to receive her benefits. So in due time, in sweet memory of her hall of fame struggles, my hope is that her grand's and great grand's reap her harvest, and receive her inheritance. Profusely, I traveled with seniors many places, by cars and vans to Little Rock AR., Memphis and Nashville TN., and Birmingham AL, just to name a few. These are truly blessings from God, to express these things in my writings; the purified truth; abundantly reminiscing on a song a writer penned, "Kept by God." We were not surprised, for the cause.

God is not through with me yet. I sense very good things in the plight and struggles of black farmers and their heirs, revealed by Him. My hope is that we might recruit young heirs to rethink and reinvestigate the plight of black farmers today by "Looking to Jesus." They are heirs of His promises. Our fathers, mothers, grand's great grand's, etc., were discriminated against, but God has the first and last words even during their generation. Today I thank God. Many young folks voluntarily worked hard to help President Obama win the race to the White House. He is a fair blessed man indeed. For monies lay in the treasure chest, hold infinite funds available to His heirs.

A young white journalist took pictures of us while walking and singing in the rain in Washington D.C. She worked for an environmental agency in that city. I asked if I could call her after returning home to Arkansas. She handed me a business card. As a result, I followed up with a phone call, to be told she could not release her findings until the year 2006, due to it being a private agency. The year Senator Obama signed the Nutritional Food Stamp Act, included Black Farmers, I believe, showed 20.5 billion dollars funded.

The God of Abraham, Isaac and Jacob blessed in Him, Paul said:

> "I think myself happy." **Acts 26:2,** he sat facing the king and, "Then King Agrippa said to Paul, You almost persuaded me to become a Christian, Paul said I would to God that not only you but also all who hear me today might become both almost and altogether such as I am, except for these chains." **Verses 28-29**

A young lady recorded a song titled: "The Chains Are Loose," I believe. It reminds me of this very verse above, as a man of freedom penned: "His Father Died Waiting, His Grand Father, Died Waiting, His Great Grand Father Died waiting,"

We are alive today waiting in hope, and in the faith of God for our inheritances. Amazingly, a judge denied our claims, our hope in God lives on as does Obamacare and it is a good thing; an Affordable Care Insurance plan to invest in healthy benefits for life. There's a word going around America in private and in public, President Obama and Vice President Biden desires great jobs that pay great benefits for all people and it is absolutely a good thing.

Again, seven years, I believe, the law of the land works today. Moses said, being the LORD's release, we are Jews or Gentiles. Whereas, I believe black's fifty years old should be paid as others, at least 50,000 dollars; especially people of Arkansas, Tenseness, Mississippi, Georgia, Alabama, and Louisiana that have worked fifty years under paid even much longer. it's on record verses others. Again, it is great to debate Civil Right's economy-wise, because cash monies would help the rich get richer, help middle-class citizens prosper again, and God's release to the poor outcast people below poverty level; beloved of God to "Shop Around."

A song writer wrote, "Joy Bells Will Be Ringing." It feels like Christmas time in the city, to lift up Jesus. In Him is a small thing for God to do in the first place. Politics and people change; God changes not. Isaiah recorded the purified Word.

> "For unto us a Child is born, unto us a Son is given, and the government will be upon His shoulder. And His name shall be called Wonderful, Counselor, Mighty God, Everlasting Father, Prince of Peace," **Isaiah 9:6. See Leviticus 25:10**.

A song writer penned, "A Message from the LORD," reminds me of a deacon in a big city who said, when it was time to pay us, discriminated against, they changed lawyers.

He knew the truth. They met many years. The same thing happened continuously, yet the deacon said, one lawyer that was fair dwell in a big city, desired one-million dollars for all without impartially. For example, God recruited Jesus His heir.

"When He was twelve years old:" **Luke 2:42**.

it feels like a Christmas Gift. Our dear sweet mother said, it's a poor wind that never changes.

"God is Judge He pulls down one and set up another." **Psalm 75:7**.

Having been a widow for years, I sense a parable; a hall of fame excellent true story.

"Then He spoke a parable to them that men always ought to pray and not lose heart, Saying: There was in a certain city; a judge who did not fear God nor regard man. Now there was a widow in that certain city; and she came to him saying, Get justice for me from my adversary: And he would not for a while; but afterward he said within himself," **Luke 18:1-4a.** Jesus expertly mastered justice.

Many years ago, a lawyer was appointed over a small inheritance to us three widowed sisters, who were indeed minding our own business. Our God revealed a small will our uncle and aunt had included us in to be split evenly. It wasn't easy work dealing with a niece as executor. So after many months, God revealed to me that I should ask my two sisters to agree with me in likeness of a widow's request, and pray for cash money, because the lawyer said the land was useless. Also she made mention of a Cadillac and some other things. The three of us lived in different places same as her niece whom our aunt appointed executive. The lawyer wrote, the will would lay in probate court for years which we knew was not fair. We agreed on the money, the unjust judge testified.

> "Though I do not fear God nor regard man, yet this widow troubles me I will avenge her lest her continued coming she weary me. Then the LORD said, Hear what the unjust judge said." **Verses 4b-6,** so questions were asked and recorded, I rewrite them saying. "And shall God not avenge His own elect who cry out day and night to Him, though He bears long with them? I tell you that He will avenge them speedily. Nevertheless, when, the Son of Man comes, will He really find faith on the earth?" **Verses 7-8**

Then it happened. Jesus tested their behavior pattern in a large crowd.

> "Said to them, which of you shall l have a friend and go to him at midnight and say to him, friend, lend me three loaves; for a friend of mine has come to me on a journey, I have nothing to set before him; and he will answer from within and say, do not trouble me; the door is now shut, and my children are now with me in bed." **Luke 11:5-7a**.

Jesus illustrates a friend's specific needs at the midnight hour said:

> "I cannot rise and give to you**? Verse 7b.**

These last seven words remind me of a play, *Certain Seasons*, when Jesus said:

> "I say to you, though he will not rise and give to him because he is his friend, yet because of his

persistence he will rise and give him as many as he needs." **Verse 8**.

A young lady said a man taught her persistence, because she needed a pen to file an application for an apartment, but she did not have a pen. She asked the man to lend her a pen. He asked where her pen was. She left to get a pen. But when she returned, she discovered her case was closed. The man didn't expect her to come back and because another lady was prepared it was given to her. Through it all, she asked to file an application. Persistence works, as it is displayed when Jesus said.

> "Ask and it will be given to you; seek and you will find; knock and it will be opened to you. If a son asks for bread from any father among you, will he give him a stone? Or if he ask for a fish, will he give him a serpent instead of a fish? Or if he ask for an egg, will he offer him a scorpion?" **Luke 11:9b-12**.

Jesus has ways to openly test us so then it is a true saying,

> "If you then, being evil, know how to give good gifts to your children, how much more will your heavenly Father give the Holy Spirit to those who ask Him?" **V 13**.

Jesus was showed a place of demons. Demons are real spirits, we know. Yet, who wants to think on devils?

> "And He was casting out a demon, and it was mute. So it was when the demon had gone out, the mute spoke and the multitude marveled. But some of them said He casts out demons by Beelzebub, the

ruler of the devils: Others testing Him sought from Him a sign from heaven," **Verses 14-16**.

Miraculously, it is not a surprise at all to His believers. What we see is what reality in our lives says.

> "But He knowing their thoughts, said to them: Every kingdom divided against itself is brought to desolation, and a house divided against itself falls;" **verse 17**.

Again two choices are revealed to us Jesus said:

> "He who is not with Me, is against Me, and he who does not gather with Me scatters" **Verse 23.**

Miraculous, a writer penned a song to help us: "When in Doubt or Distress Talk It over with Jesus."

> "And it happened, as He spoke these things, a certain woman from the crowd raised her voice and said to Him: Blessed is the womb that bore You, and the breasts which nursed You! But He said, More than that, blessed are those who hear the word of God and keep it" **Verses 27-28**.

Blessed are we for the wind blows dry leaves east, west, north and south; especially in between summer and autumn.

Glancing back at our supernatural days at Wonder Junior High, a few of us discovered we could sing as we listened to the radio. Back then we practiced and sang a supernatural song titled, I believe, "Anyway the Wind Blows Its Cool with Me." A few of us had it going on. We practiced singing together, and could have made it big had we an expert to train us. I believe we would have produced supernatural records specialized in songs big time, since some of us sung in junior choirs, within our churches, and **Wonder**'s choir. A top music teacher expertly trained her choir; accepted or rejected, "Less than our best is failure." A good friend tried out for Mrs. T's choir. She said her voice could cause her choir to crack up, because her voice was not meant for singing.

She was right. We laughed in self pity, because God's mercies hid our misery. Mrs. T lived a blessed life. In memory of **Wonder**'s best music teacher, a writer penned, "I Have Decided to Follow Jesus, No Turning Back:"

> "When an innumerable multitude of people had gathered together; so that they trampled one another, He began to say to His disciples, first of all beware of the leaven of the Pharisees which is hypocrisy," **Luke 12:1**.

I always think about what Jesus said; pass it on and pass on the way to fear Him, because,

> "There is nothing covered that shall not be revealed neither hid that shall not be known. Therefore whatsoever you have spoken in darkness shall be heard in the light; and that which you have spoken in the ear in closets shall be proclaimed on the housetop." **Verses 2-3,**

Suddenly, at a wedding reception, a man said within our hearing, "You can't play with God, I know what Jesus said.

> "But I will show you whom you should fear. Fear Him who, after He has killed, has power to cast into hell; yes I say fear Him!" **verse 5.**

I found out the man's wife was my former classmate. We grew up on the south side of town. She said her husband was a faithful husband and father to their children. Years later he passed away. In memory of her husband, "We can't play with God". Joel means Jehovah is God; he stuck to his assignment passed onward.

> "Tell your children about it, let your children tell their children, and their children another generation" **Joel 1:3**.

"Be Careful Little Ears What You Hear; Be Careful Little Eyes What You See; Be Careful Little Mouth What You Speak; If You Want To Walk Like Jesus."

Amazingly, a few women from church attended a conference and invested in the evidence planned to encourage young people to work together. They trained a Good Samaritan; a little boy on fire for God. Amazingly, he learned the works. He marched, praised God in Scriptures, stirred up the church. Their eyes opened, by the power of God's blessings and wonders.

At 3:00 a.m. I had a vision on a Tuesday morning in the year 2002. Printed on my bedroom closet door; same as written in my Bible, with one hand and one finger pointed to words on my door, my other hand covered my mouth. I stood unaware of getting out of bed, but I read:

> "And Jesus answering and said unto them have faith in God. For verily I say to you; That whosoever shall say unto this mountain Be thou removed, and be thou cast into the sea; and shall not doubt in his heart, but shall believe that those things which he

said shall come to pass; he shall have whatsoever he said." **Mark 11:22-23**.

I reread three verses where Jesus said:

> "Therefore I say to you, what things so ever you desire, when you pray, believe that you receive them and you shall have them." **Verse 24.**

God said to me, there's more to come. I was utterly wide awake; wondering what was going on. My husband was totally disabled for fourteen years, and the last five, he could not move his feet side to side back or forward. But by the power of God invested within me, I was able to take of him totally. At 8:00 a.m., God said turn on your T.V. An opened Bible faced my screen, with Mark 11:22-26 displayed. A preacher preached a double sermon. I've never forgotten it. It was titled, "Have Faith in God;" "Be Silent No More", showed on T.V. plus:

> "And when you stand praying forgive, if you have aught against any: that your Father also which is in heaven may forgive your trespasses: But if you do not forgive, neither will your Father which is in heaven forgive your trespasses." **Verses 25-26**

Jesus forgives. Since He excuses our sins, faith and forgiveness work together. A week later, my husband felt warm and I called my younger daughter, a nurse. She came over and checked his temperature; it was very high. But he had a doctor's appointment that day and my eldest daughter's husband, my son-in-law said, he would take him. I was sick, but the plan was already inaction. When his doctor examined him, my son-in-law telephoned to say Joe was too weak to hold his head up.

I called my daughter and explained what happened. She called his doctor who said Joe should be hospitalized. He said no rooms were available in the hospital, but nurses and doctors talks the same talk. They discovered a room and checked him in the place. April 03, 2002 God awaken me from sleep at 3:00 a.m. and said, "go see Joe." I said LORD I'm unable to drive; He said, "I will take care of you." I entered Joe's room at 7:00 a.m. leaned on the door, then walked to his bed, hugged him, and asked how he felt. Joe said, "I'm sick." I responded by saying, ask God to help you, and He will; just believe.

Shortly after that, a group of doctors entered his room asking questions. I was thankful they came in while I was present in the room, because he didn't feel up to answer their questions. So when they left, he was satisfied. Later on that day, he said, "you can go, I will be alright." I returned home called his brother to see if he'd sit with him, and he said yes. Then I was satisfied. The next day April 04, 2002 at 3:00 a.m. a nurse called from the hospital asked if this was Mrs. Andrews. I said yes. She said Mr. Andrews had just expired. I said Joe couldn't be dead, I just saw him on yesterday. She asked if I had someone to bring me to the hospital. I said yes, my daughter.

Reflecting back, I believe Joe knew. He released me the day, before he passed away; saying "I will be all right now." Joe was stricken with something akin to muscular dystrophy. That condition Jerry Lewis campaigned for on T.V. God enabled me to go see my husband a day before he

slipped away. I have always been grateful to Him for that.
Later on, his doctor said had he survived, his failure to
breathe on his own would have caused him to enter a
nursing home. He was too proud for that. God knows best.
One thing I know, if we do our best, rain or shine, He will
absolutely carry us through the storms of life, only if we
believe. God is able. I continue to cling to His blessings.

Even today, throughout trials that is life, yet my writing and
rewriting my God breathed book, works wonders for me.
Because He captures my attention more abundantly beyond
my wisest dreams or visions, three books are already set up
to write God willing. He is my hope in that all the glory
belongs to Him. Since I cannot write books without His
divine power, "less than our best is failure." God awakened
me one morning and said **Psalm 12:6**. I opened my Bible
and read:

>"The words of the LORD are pure words: Like
>silver tried in a furnace of earth, purified seven
>times," verse 6. Then: "You shall keep them LORD,
>You shall preserve from this generation forever."
>**Verse 7**.

A woman of faith said she read her Bible three times a
week. Influenced by, God I said try to read it every day.
Joy was in her voice.

>"For the Holy Spirit will teach you in that very hour
>what you ought to say." **Luke 12:12** "Looking to
>Jesus;" "Then one from the crowd said to Him
>Teacher, tell my brother to divide the inheritance
>with me. But He said to him, Man Who made Me a

judge or arbitrator over you? And He said to them, take heed and beware of covetousness, for one's life does not consist in the abundance of the things he possesses." **Verses 13-15**

Remarkably, Jesus abundantly shows a way to reap and sow in His remarks:

> "He spoke a parable to them, saying: the ground of a certain rich man yielded plentifully. And he thought within himself, saying what shall I do since I have no room to store my crops? So he said, I will do this: I will pull down my barns and build greater and there I will store all my crops and my goods." **Verses 16-18**

 I recall our grand's kept the four of us busy, but in this parable a rich man tested failure, because the more he had the more he desired to have. He said this:

> "I will say to my soul, Soul, you have many goods laid up for many years take your ease, eat, drink and be merry;" verse **19**.

Memories of our grand's chores and tasks were burden bearers. My twin brother and I worked together outwardly; fed the hog, chickens, and tried milking a cow, within our hometown of West Memphis, Arkansas. And we kept the yards swept clean before age eleven. Our two sisters worked within the house, yet the four of us worked. Had we worked our children today likewise, we would've been arrested; charged with child abuse. Because someone would tell on Face book, twitter, email or snap pictures on I phone. Solomon wrote and God's revelations confirmed these things.

> "To everything there is a season, and a time to every purpose under heaven" **Ecclesiastes 3:1.**

Remember nothing is hidden from Him, not even the privacy act, because He knows spies personally.

> "God said to him, fool this night your soul will be required of you; then whose will those things be which you have provided?" **Luke 12:20.**

Growing up within our grand's house, they taught us to give, but it was no credit to us. We had no choice and their orders worked. For example, in those days we hand delivered fresh vegetables to the widows in our neighborhood. Even when papa slaughtered his hog in the wintertime, we hand delivered fresh pork on our two feet. The hard work developed our character. Jesus declared:

> "So who lays up treasures for himself, and is not rich toward God. Then He said to His disciples, therefore I say to you, do not worry about your life, what you will eat; nor about the body, what you will put on." **Verses 21-22**

Now I know why papa didn't worry. Fresh meat hung in his smokehouse; peaches, apples, etc., canned in jars kept in closets and under their bed. Our grandmother cooked fat of hogs that cleaned like brand name all-purposed cleansers do today. And papa, who was a Sunday school superintendent, in Jericho Arkansas, dressed superbly; lacking nothing when he attended church. Oh yes, and he

served years in our hometown of West Memphis as a
deacon. He liked to fish, hunt and read the *Memphis Press*.
Papa liked to watch pretty women walk our street too. It is
a fact, because, "Papa Was a Rolling Stone." But Papa
ruled his house; the four of us had clothes on our backs
shoes on our feet, which never wore out.

We worked the fields carrying water in a tin bucket that
people drank from, using the same long handled dipper.
After watching some of the elders dip bitter stuff in the heat
of the day, and used the same long handle dipper, no
wonder elders said to feed your enemies with a long
handled spoon. Then it happened. A song writer penned the
song "It's good to Know Jesus." So,

> "Then Peter said to Him, LORD, do You speak this
> parable only to us, or to all people? And the LORD
> said, who then is that faithful and wise steward,
> whom his master will make ruler over his household
> to give their potion of food in due season." **Luke
> 12:41-42**.

A certain former classmate of **Wonder**, who worked hard
to earn her degree, married, moved to a big city and made it
to the top in her chosen career. In time, she returned to our
hometown, purchased a home and continued to work.
Today, she enjoys God's blessings and celebrates her
promotion. She joyously 'shook the shackles off her feet.'
I, along with a few of **Wonder**'s former classmates, joined
in, and we all shook 'shackles' off our feet to help celebrate
her God given blessings according to His Word.

> "Blessed is that servant whom his master will find
> so doing when He comes. Truly, I say to you that he

will make him ruler over all that he has." **Luke 12:43-44**.

My former classmate attended New St. Paul Church with us way before our school of **Wonder** was built. Back then we wore black and brown oxfords that never wore out. Moses wrote **Deuteronomy 29:5** which embraces God's blessings, as President Obama spoke great and mighty blessings with ability under God, in the highest position. Moses said:

> "The secret things belong to the LORD our God, but those things which are revealed belong to us and our children forever; that we may do all the work of the law." **Deuteronomy 29:29**. "For Jesus Himself testified that a prophet has no honor in his own country. So when He came to Galilee, the Galileans received Him, having seen all the things He did in Jerusalem at the feast; for they also had gone to the feast." **John 4:44-45**.

Chapter Three
"Great and Mighty Things"

> "Moreover the Word of the LORD came to
> Jeremiah a second time while he was still shut in the
> court of the prison, saying: Thus says the LORD
> who made it, the LORD who formed it to
> established it the LORD is His name." **Jeremiah
> 33:1-2.**

One evening our witness team was invited to a church to
witness, pray and walk around a prison within our
hometown. Before we opened up praise and worship, I
quoted God saying:

> "Call unto Me, and I will answer you, and show you
> great and mighty things which you know not:"
> **verse 33**.

There was a lady who heard me and her face lit up in
likeness of a bright, shiny morning star. I never, ever
forgot the look on her face and I believe she did not forget
mine. God made the light to shine on us, which continues
to shine, even when we cannot look up and see His sun
moon or stars. He is everywhere. Moreover, I value and
titled my third chapter in special honor to God, because
whenever I see 333 on my clock, I quote and meditate on
His great and mighty invitation, which delights me inward
and outward.

Awesomely, I asked God where to go from here. Gazing at
verses 4-5, causes me to remember down time, a reminder
that His restoration act is next on line; for He is always on

time and owns time. So I see health insurance, peace, truth and His divine promises saying:

> "Behold, I will bring them the abundance of peace and truth:" **Verse 6**.

So I use my God given time, and offer great mighty sacrifice of praises to Him; a declaration of independence, peace and truth met together as promised by God, Himself with great and mighty blessings.

***

I greet former staff who worked for East Central Arkansas E.D.C. agency housed in Forrest City Arkansas. I make mention of former staff in my book; first in memories of all agency staff that have passed away. I acknowledge former executives, supervisors, site directors, assistants directors, van drivers, chefs, title five, senior workers, black caucus, and volunteers, within three to five county service areas. God rest their souls.

Secondly, the class action lawsuit filed October 1997 failed on July 03, 2013. A few of us were in Court to hear the end results; some staff and others who did not know the facts. A few former staff persons continued to call to ask questions, so I thought it appropriate to share the true facts.

The sixteen year class action lawsuit failed, because our two private lawyers failed to certify our case in court. Some of the staff said we should've filed complaints against the two private lawyers. It was said that one of the lawyers had faced the board before. I responded: Anyone is welcome to proceed with the sixteen year lawsuit, but as for me, I called the lawyer's office tried to get information, and I wasn't the only one to call them regularly. I thought we should know these great and mighty things. Yet on behalf of former staff, God blessed us to work years for these people under the agency, to serve three to five counties well. Although the agency was insured, for whatever things went wrong, far as I know we were innocent and did not receive our benefits, after three judges, four lawyers, with two remaining on the case. Had it not been God on our side, the entire staff would not have been paid September 01 thru September 15, 1997.

Unfortunately, because the agency closed without notice on payday, I called the county Judge in Forrest City to ask for help for all ECA's staff, and he agreed to meet with me. I'm sure the county judge knew ahead of time about our situation. The staff only found out that same day. A site director and I were with our senior citizens touring the state of Texas and had returned that same day. The judge called the bank and our checks were approved with the bookkeepers doing the rest. So I make mention of ECA in by book, because a person from the agency made it to Forrest City too late to cash his paycheck, so one check bounced.

Being director at that time, I suffered down time as he did. If God is willing, I will reimburse him; having known the young man from childhood, through church and our school of **Wonder**. However, he was faithful. It soothed my spirit to offer help, knowing God works wonders. I called the county clerk at the courthouse, who said our case was on docket with a case number, and I passed it on. The agency's lawyers reported in court that three years of Social Security had not been paid by ECA for staff at that time. Staff persons suffering illnesses filed health claims that were useless. Ninety-five percent black employed regardless of color, gender, creed sunshine or rain. That staff moved and served all approved of services, within the poorest counties. The results were wonderful to serve them yet we wondered. Paul wrote:

> "But we have this treasure in earthen vessels that the excellence of the power may be of God and not us. We are hard pressed on every side yet not crushed; we are perplexed, but not in despair, persecuted, but not forsaken, struck down, but not destroyed." **1st Corinthians 4:7-9**

In Christ, we have a wonderful working life; troubled on every side. Yet we have a Helper around the clock. Paul added:

> "Always carrying about in the dying of our LORD Jesus Christ, that the life of Jesus also may be manifested in our bodies**;" verse 10**. "Therefore we do not lose heart: even though our outward man is perishing, yet the inward man is being renewed day by day." **Verse 16**.

So I stick to God's blessings in honor to His Anointed Specialist. Favorably the psalmist declared, and I act upon the words:

> "In You O LORD, I put my trust; Let me never be put to shame. Deliver me in Your righteousness, and cause me to escape; Incline Your ear to me, and save me. Be my strong refuge to which I may resort continually you have given the commandment to save me: For You are my rock and my fortress." **71:1-3a**.

The evidence says:

> "Deliver me, O LORD God, out of the hand of the
> wicked, out of the hand of the unrighteous and cruel
> man. For you are my hope; O LORD God: You are
> my trust from my youth," **Verse 3b-5**.

To all former staff, we left the agency empty handed, yet I
remain filled with hope in Him. As for me, I said to an
elderly lady and a younger lady, both staff, I was going to
make mention of these things within my book, which is the
absolute truth. A certain Judge promised in court, June 16,
2009, in our presence that he was a Christian, a deacon in
his church; he knew what we were going through in that
place of justice.

In all we did, we sincerely believed him. We believed we
would receive our benefits since county Judges served on
ECA'S Broad of Directors in the counties we served. They
always said we served all clients very well, so it wasn't fair
we were sold out. Then the Judge told lawyers to have
evidence on his desk within sixty days or get ready for
court December 2009. That absolutely lifted up our down
time!

Then a lawyer told us, the Court had a murder trial that
month. The judge appointed a young white lady to speak
for us. The same young lady that hand delivered forms to
me for the Aging staff to file. At this time, we had four
lawyers. Then I hand delivered the forms to all the Aging
staff; picked up the completed forms; and hand delivered
them to the lawyer's office in Forrest City. The young
white lady, appointed by the Judge, asked if we would
settle our cases for less than the amount we were seeking. I
told her the truth, no thanks! When we tried to reach her

later, we discovered she moved out of town, never to be heard from again.

So we never met with the first judge. The second one took on that promise to help us receive our benefits from the agency. This new judge, who was assigned to us, examined the evidence on file, on July 03, 2013, the last day in court, told us the truth. The class action lawsuit had not been certified in court. The lawyer and staff said they needed witnesses; we were the witnesses as written.

> "I have become a wonder to many, But You are my strong refuge," verse **7**.

One day, one of our bookkeepers jokingly asked, "who you think you are Jeweline?" In response, I testified, as a child of the Most High GOD favorably by HIM; my refuge same as did the psalmist says:

> "Let my mouth be filled with Your praise and with Your glory all the day. Do not cast me off in the time of old age do not forsake me when my strength fails" verses **8-9**.

I found out the executive director that hired me passed away. But before he died, he shared with a family friend the reason he hired me. I was to become Aging director at the time appointed, but first I was a volunteer, delivering meals to 60+ plus home bound seniors in my hometown. Then one of our former **Wonder** students informed me a data clerk was need while she was coordinator at the senior center.

In that, the same exec hired me as data clerk before he passed, his prophesy was right on time. I was hired as Aging director, because it was God's will spoken by a man of faith. May God bless the staff who worked at ECA. It's a joy having worked with people willing to serve others, big time!

Notably, a lady wrote a song called, "A Second Time." I recall a former classmate of mine who was taller than me. Because she grew up with three strong brothers to fight for her, no one tackled us. When she was of age, she moved to a big city, married, and had children before returning to our hometown for a short visit with her son. He told her had he lived back then in that house they grew up in, he would have killed himself. I said to myself, he would have missed how amazingly the Almighty God blessed us to live in brick houses with one or more bathrooms inward, and not outward. In God's care, we cannot go backward today.

Her son had no clue that even in hard times, we didn't know we were poor, since we enjoyed everything fresh from the ground to eat. We never even heard of cholesterol, a fatty crystalline substance derived from bile, known as a bitter yellow or greenish liquid secreted by the liver. Unlike today, we had no physician. He blessed us to stay well. Parents today are free to choose and invest in Obamacare with pre-existing illnesses approved. Students attending college can remain insured through their parents' plan till age twenty-six. Uninsured young people are able to 'shop around' for a plan suitable to their needs.

For example, during our youth, we could smell fresh greens cooking before we entered our gate. Just like Papa's German shepherd, fenced in under his house, warned him if anyone approached the gate. Or like a scarecrow scared birds from their garden. This caused me to wonder, how on earth did a dressed up stick with a hat on top make a fool out of birds? In fact, it is a riddle, how the two of them made asafetida bags to tie around our necks to keep us healthy. The smell may have made me ill, yet kept us well.

Back then, we enjoyed a taste of humor from time to time. A few of us loved peeping in the windows at a certain drug store, where little white children sat on bar stools at the counter sipping cokes. One day, a genius we called an expert, said we should walk to the druggist on Broadway and sit on those stools and order cokes. So four or five of us went along with his plan and did just that. After all, he was the one with money to buy cokes for us, so we followed his lead. He had money, because his mom was a long termed school teacher, and his dad was a big time doctor. God smiled on us and kept us safe.

But they did not serve us. We were asked to leave and told by a white man not to come back no more. Had our folks found out, imagine the scene in our houses. The song, "its Not Just My Imagination", came to mind looking at the owner's face in that drug store. It was fun for us to see, because we were children at the time and all things were funny.

We laughed like we did when a favorite classmate of my oldest sister, had us laughing, when we walked from school. He was a famed comedian though he died before he journeyed to Hollywood to try out for those comedy shows. In memory, he was one of a kind; a **Wonder** lion.

There was a famous woman who sang sweet true words; "Nobody Knows the Troubles I've Seen, Nobody Knows, But Jesus." We may have had some troubles, yet we had some good days too! After our sweet, dear mother past away, the four of us would've flunked growing up. But a man called Jesus ruled in our favor. My dear readers, I've never forgotten Him. For we escaped being separated one from another.

An inspired thought crept in my spirit, as a certain journalist reported on T.V, about a politician who concerned himself with political matters. What he said made sense, at such times as this. The politician said, "Many people have to work longer and harder than others before they retire, since job descriptions shows they hold tougher positions." For example: Home health-aids, city workers, clerks, etc., constantly make the poor comfortable, manifest the truth on purpose. Yet the poor people who chopped, picked, and pulled cotton many years with the land owners failing to invest in benefits like Social Security etc.

> "Jesus answering and said to him, Blessed are you Simon Bar-Jonah, for flesh and blood has not revealed this to you, but My Father who is in heaven. And I also say to you that you are Peter, and on this rock I will build My church, and the gates of Hades shall not prevail against it." **Matthew 16: 17-18**.

God's truth is within the heart.

> "And He will give you the keys of the kingdom of heaven and whatever you bind on earth will be

bound in heaven, and whatever you loose on earth will be loosed in Heaven." Verse **19**

Three way plans are in order: Father, Son and Holy Spirit working on earth together.

"Then He commanded His disciples that they should tell no one that He was Jesus the Christ" verse **20; see 21-28**.

President Obama and Vice President Biden work together to keep America safe. God hold keys to the world in His hand. Peter said,

"Obey God rather than man," a taste of **Acts 5:29**.

These great things remind me of an elderly woman during our Sunday school hour. She spoke like God was the head of her table. She constantly reminded the senior adult class to trust God always instead of man. A friend called me while I was deleting hundreds of pages within my book in which has become habitually but not on purpose, because we were taught "Less than our best is failure." To tell us the truth, I have to obey the voice of God that speaks to me being the One that continue to talk to me. Amazingly He equips someone like me to continue to write is amazing. "Let the LORD be glorified." His Old and New Testament characters reveal true stories as well as true characters. God reminded me of a certain rich man, who was a big time leader in a big time city, who got caught up with the cares of the world. But he confessed his sins in private, even in a crowd place. The man showed good character traits, because it is true when Jesus said:

"For everyone in whom much is given, from him much is required;" Luke 12:48b. See requirements vv 48c-59. Then obey: "Jesus said I tell you, no, but unless you repent you will all likewise perish," **Luke 13:5.**

Whereas two pathways manifests the verbs to repent or perish; it is a choice saying.

"He also spoke a parable; a certain man had a fig tree in his vineyard and he came seeking fruit on it and found none. Then he said to the keeper of his vineyard, Look, for three years I have come seeking fruit on this fig tree and find none. Cut it down; why does it use up the ground?" **Verses 6-7.**

Jesus' parables are bold'

"But he answered and said to him, Sir let it alone this year also until I dig around it and fertilize it. And if it bears fruit, well. But after that you can cut it down." verses **8-9.**

It's true the keeper asked for more time to work, and taught him to ask.

"Now He was teaching in one of the synagogues on the Sabbath. And behold, there was a woman, who had a spirit of infirmity eighteen years and she was bent over and could in no way raise herself up. But when Jesus saw her and He called her to Him and said to her, woman you are loosed from your infirmity." Vv 10-12 Then a miracle happened Jesus touched; "And He laid His Hands on her immediately she was made straight and glorified God." **Verse 13.**

Imagine, if one beloved family member or myself, walked bent over for eighteen years, and suddenly on a Sabbath Day, with just a little talk with Jesus made her walk straight, as He healed her instantly.

> "But the ruler of the synagogue answered with indignation, because Jesus had healed on the Sabbath; and he said to the crowd; there are six days on which men ought to work; therefore come and be healed on them, and not on the Sabbath." **Verse 14.**

Ultimately, Jesus has first and last words

> "The LORD then answered and said, Hypocrite! Does not each of you on the Sabbath loose his ox or donkey from the stall, and lead it away to water it; So ought this woman, being a daughter of Abraham whom Satan has bound, think, of it, for eighteen years be loosed from this bond on the Sabbath?" **Verse 15-16.**

He knew hypocrisy.

> "And when He said these things all His adversaries were put to shame; and all the multitude rejoiced for all the glorious things that were done by Him." **Verse 17**.

Jesus tested them.

> "Asked what the kingdom of God is like? And what shall I compare it? It is like a mustard seed, which a man took and put in his garden; and it grew and became a tree and the birds of the air nested in its branches." **Verses 18-19**

Again Jesus answers double questions, whether people know true or false. He speaks out any way in abundance.

> "And again He said; to what shall I liken the kingdom of God? It is like leaven, which a woman took and hid in three measures of meal till it was all leavened." **Verses 20-21**

Jesus illustrated a tiny 'mustard seed', which when it is sown in the ground is smaller than all the seeds on earth. Jesus explained in **Mark 4:30**. People grow up, as does a tiny baby in the cradle out grows his own baby crib. By faith I confess with a mustard seed of faith, God spoke plainly for the first time, "Write the book", and it was not my imagination. I knew it wasn't over yet. But responded, LORD, I'm not even a good speller; nor do I connect my nouns and verbs to create good sentences to write a book. God said two of your nephews write. I was amazed He shared a taste of their story.

I passed on to each of them great things God said to me, without a response in return. But one thing I know, years later, one wrote a book of poems; and he writes a book today. I did not hear a word from God, but I knew my joy was not hidden, because I told everyone; my family, extended family and whosoever listened. My eldest sister was so excited; she sent newspaper clippings from Flint Michigan with a picture of a young lady who had just written her first book. I was very encouraged and never forgot her wonder working words to someone like me. I said to an elderly friend, it is too hard to write. I was not complaining, for it is one of the best things I have ever tried to do, I can't thank Him enough for selecting me to write.

Before I completed my sentence the elder said, if it was too easy it probably wouldn't be God. August 18, 2001, the second time God said write, the book, I was not surprised at all, certainly not. He said title your book: *The Way of Escape*. **2nd Peter 1:4**. In awe, I said wow! I was extremely excited and did not expect Him to provide a titled for my book, although I knew He would speak to me again. God is my witness; I reread mighty ways to escape failure saying,

> "Whereby are given unto us exceedingly great and precious promises: that by these you might be partakers of the divine nature having escape the corruption that is in the world through lust" **2nd Peter 1:4**.

A great and mighty song leapt within my spirit, in memory of a great song, "It's been a Long Time Coming, But a Change Is Going To Come." So be it. Is anyone ready to give up on a God given assignments or task? We might fail at first, but He doesn't. Young or old believe the truth; a writer wrote a song that introduced wonder in Him, like a breath of fresh autumn air with a touch of winter's cold air. "What a Mighty God We Serve."

God kept saying write the book. He said don't worry about the publisher. I told many people. Some wrote books; some said they were going to write a book. Another lady shared her title with me; she was absolutely excited. At last, a lady said she heard me say God said write a book. She wondered if I knew what I had gotten myself into. I responded, God said write the book not me.

"God is not a man, that He should lie, nor a son of man that should repent: Has He said and will not do it? Or has He spoken and will He not make it good?" **Numbers 23:19** And He affirmed again: "In hope of eternal life which God, who cannot lie promised before time began, but has in due time manifested His Word through preaching to the commandment of God our Savior." **Titus 1:2-3**.

Excitedly, it is truly quite honorable writing, praying, praising and worshiping God at this time in my life. A song writer wrote, and a lady sang it affirmed. "Count Your Blessings One By One." I said to our God in wonder, LORD help me Jesus.

A young lady attended a black farmers meeting, same as did I one Saturday morning, at a church in Memphis TN. Suddenly, standing outside after the meeting, she came over to the place I stood and said she had just written and self published a child's book. She signed her book and handed me a copy. Then said God told her to give me a copy of her book. I had never laid eyes on her. I looked at her book and asked her how much do I owed you? She said it was mine. The lady with me looked amazed as I accepted her gift. She was sent by God as another confirmation.

Notably, it was a beautiful, bright, hot orange colored book kids would love. I still hold on to my book, as a miraculous sign from heaven above. I believed every one of God's wonder working, hall of fame wonders in heaven and on His earth.

For example, I wondered, as a writer wrote and sang, "Whose That Lady." April 04, 2003, one year after my husband passed away, a group of women from different churches journeyed to Bagdad Kentucky. It was their 11th Annual Christian Ladies Retreat. Then it happened. With a tablet on hand and pen in my hand, I begin writing great things to the glory of God I penned that same day and hour as it is recorded saying.

> "In the beginning God created the heavens and the earth. The earth was without form, and void; and darkness was on the face of the deep. And the Spirit of God moved upon the face of the waters. And God saw the light that it was good; and God divided the light from the darkness." **Genesis 1:1-4**.

Writing and deleting from that day forward, I completed my first book on June 16, 2004. I asked my cousin, and former **Wonder** student to edit it for me. She was experienced in her work, but she had just retired. Then I asked if she knew anyone that might edit my book. She knew a couple of Christian ladies that might help me. She gave me their telephone numbers. The first lady I called was sick. The second lady agreed to edit my book, if I was not in a hurry. I sent my disk; ready to pay upon her request, the amount, but in no hurry. She called once to ask a question. I answered and she seemed satisfied. Her being an experienced editor, I was glad to hear from her.

So, about fourteen months later, on August 09, 2005, I called her. I stated my name and titled of my book and asked how she was coming along with it. She responded, "oh yes, the escape." Then she explained how she purchased a new computer and may have lost my disk. She asked if I would hold on while she checked. I waited and waited. She did not return to the telephone. Then God said to me quietly; said do not worry, because they forgot Joseph, but I didn't nor his biological father. I hung up my telephone worry free, because I believed, received and accepted His divine words about His servant Joseph, revealed to me that day of fame.

I did not call the expert lady again, nor did she return my call; nor was I angry with her, although I remember every word she spoke. It was because of her expressions were; their first grand baby arrived on earth so be it. A few days later, four ladies from the same church attended a Sprit filled conference in the great city of Atlanta. Excellent speakers lifted up Jesus. We returned home, renewed in spirit. I resumed writing my book. Thinking again, the lady pastor was right, it wasn't easy to record a book when Jesus says write it. A song writer penned, "Holy, holy, holy, LORD God, Almighty, Who was and is to come!" Revealed, also in **Revelation 4:8b**

I completed my book again on June 21, 2006. This time with a contract between us, I mailed my disk, and amount agreed upon to an expert well known publisher. In the fullness of God's glory, I was greatly satisfied with our contract. Seven days later my work returned to me by express mail. I opened up my work and at first glimpse, it was marked up badly. It was hard for me to believe experts work like that. I called on God to help me and He quieted my spirit, then I called the agency and asked for the representative by name. She had quit. But that's not the way my true story ended, I prayed fervently asking God to help me.

I spoke to the editor, who had been promoted to Executive Manager. I explained the above situation and we talked back and forth. He wanted to send half of my money, which wasn't fair, because I paid for the entire packaged deal. So then I asked for the owner. He agreed, reimbursed my money in full. I told him I understood why he was promoted. I ask that God keep on blessing this woman of faith, because I trust Him, who promoted you as well someone like me that fully believe He is the joy of my life.

Incredibly, God revealed my favorite salvation story by His incredible grace through the most popular game on earth, hide and seek.

> "And He entered a house and wanted no one to know it, but He could not be hidden. For a woman whose young daughter had an unclean spirit heard about Him, she came and fell at His feet: The woman was a Greek, a Syro-Phoenician by birth, and she kept asking Him to cast the demon out of her daughter" **Mark 7:24a-26**.

I bowed on my knees; offering thanks to God, having reread the woman's needs many times. I share this with many. The woman knew who to contact. He couldn't hide, because her only daughter needed deliverance from a demon, just right for Jesus to heal her.

> "But Jesus said to her let the children be fed first, for it is not good to take the children's bread and throw it to the little dogs. And she answered and said to Him, Yes LORD, yet even the little dogs under the table eat from the children's crumbs. Then He said to her, for these sayings go your way; the demon has gone out of your daughter."
> **Verses 27-29**

But in due respect to Jesus, her God given act of faith worked blessings for the two of them. She caught up with Him; challenged God straight into the hall of fame

> "When she had come to her house: she found the demon gone out and her daughter lying on the bed." **verse 30**.

The woman may have heard that Jesus made a way of escape for the two of them it is written.

> "Beyond measure, saying He had done all things well. He makes both the deaf to hear and the mute to talk," **verse 37b**.

Moving forward, we see glimpses of those days, when David testified with a harp in his hands; causing King Saul to quiet with great and mighty results. David wrote:

> "O LORD, You have searched me and known me. You know my sitting down and my rising up; you understand my thoughts afar off You comprehend my path and my lying down, And are acquainted with all my ways: For there in not a word on my tongue. But behold, O LORD, You know it altogether." **Psalm 139:1-4.**

Glory to God he confessed.

> "You hedge me behind and before: And laid Your hands on me. Such knowledge is too wonderful for me: it is high, I cannot attain it. Where shall I go from Your Spirit? Or where can I flee from Your presence?" **verse V7.**

There's no way anyone can hide from God.

> "If I ascend into heaven, You are there, if I make my bed in hell, behold You are there. If I take the wings of the morning and dwell in the uttermost parts of the sea: even Your hands will lead me, and your right hand will hold me" **Verses 8-10**.

A song writer penned, "Hold To God's Unchanging Hands." It is true that David spoke facts.

> "If I say, surely the darkness shall fall on me, even the night shall be light about me; indeed, the darkness shall not hide from You, but the night shines as the day: The darkness and the light are both alike to You." **Verses 11-12**

Assuredly, he had a feeling God fixed him up in his mother's womb, because he testified great things for us to copy.

> "For You formed my inwards parts; You covered me in my mother's womb. I will praise You for I am fearfully and wonderfully made. Marvelous are Your works, and my soul knows very well. My frame was not hidden from You, when I was made in secret and skillfully wrought in the lowest part of the earth." Verses **13-15**

David's words are as clear as water was created for all people to survive, same as God created Adam, when he said:

> "Your eyes saw my substance, being yet unformed. And in Your Book they all were written, the days fashion for me, when as yet there were none of

them. How precious are Your thoughts to me O God are: How great is the sum of them!" **Vv 16-17**

God revealed a young lady had cancer; a writer penned and she sang, "O How Precious Is His Name." By this time, she called Jesus three times; preciously He lives on today. David said:

> "If I should count them they would be more in number than the sand; When I awake I am still with You. O that You would slay the wicked O God! Depart from me, therefore you bloodthirsty men." **Verses 18-19** He hated evil see verses **20-22**.

David's last words in the precious chapter say:

> "Search me, O God, and know my heart; Try me, and know my anxieties; and see if there is any wicked way in me, and lead me in the way everlasting." **Verses 23-24.**

In the process of time,

> "There was a certain man in Caesarea called Cornelius, a centurion of what was called the Italian Regiment, a devout man and one that feared God with all his household, who gave much alms generously to the people and prayed to God always" **Acts 10:1-2.** It was "About the ninth hour of the day he saw clearly an angel of God saying to him Cornelius! And when he observed him, he was afraid and said what is it LORD? He said to him your prayers and your alms have come up for a memorial before God." **Verses 3-4.**

Although Cornelius was afraid, at the prime of his life, God revealed great and mighty things to him when He said:

> "Now send men to Joppa, and call one Simon a tanner whose surname is Peter: He is lodging with Simon a tanner, whose house is by the sea: He will tell you what you must do." Verses **5-6**

I believe he used a secret weapon in abundance to have prayed so fervently.

> "When the angel which spoke to him had departed Cornelius called two of his household servants and a devout soldier from among those who waited on him continually: When he had explained all these things to them, he sent them to Joppa." **Verses 7-8.**

Then it happened on site.

> "At Joppa there was a certain disciple named Tabitha, which was by interpretation called Dorcas: The woman was full of good works and charitable deeds which she did." But it happened in those days that she became sick and died. When they had washed her they laid her in the upper room." **Acts 9:36-37.**

Amazingly, supernatural joy favored God;

> "Since Lydda was near Joppa, the disciples had heard Peter was there, they sent two men to him, imploring him not to delay his coming to them," **v 38** reveals. "Then Peter arose and went with them. When he had come, they brought him to the upper room. And all the widows stood by him weeping,

showing the tunics and garments which Dorcas had made while she was with them." **Verse 39**.

I absolutely recall standing revelations, my dear readers. A former classmate of **Wonder** shared her only daughter's testimony years ago with me. She said when she started to work as an airline stewardess, before she boarded the airplane, she always said: You first Jesus then I will follow. I believe knew she could not see His footprints, high beyond His wonder clouds, but she knew God's invisible, supernatural presence was present with her, even before she was born; made in the image of God, same as Dorcas. He knows exactly everything about our past, present, and future.

> "But Peter put them all out, and knelt down and prayed. And turning to the body he said, Tabitha, arise. And she opened her eyes, and when she saw Peter she sat up. Then he gave her his hand and lifted her up, and when he called the saints and the widows, and he presented her alive:" **verses 40-41**. It was no secret God used Peter, "It became known throughout all Joppa and many believed on the LORD. So it was that he stayed many days in Joppa with Simon a tanner," **9:42-43**.

Miraculously, Peter was bold as gold shines in the sunshine. Since gender didn't matter, Dorcas received a miracle.

> "The next day, as they went on their journey and drew near the city Peter went up to the housetop to pray the sixth hour. Then he became hungry and wanted to eat; but while he made ready, he fell into a trance." **Acts 10:9-10**.

A trance is a deep sleep that moves a person out of their mind; maybe away from the pain of it all together. For example, a close family member laid in a trance to the point death. His doctor released him to a nursing home for breathing treatments. But miraculously, we continued to pray. I wrote his name in hope: "Jesus said, have faith in God." A taste of **Mark 11:22**. God called his name. With eyes open, they laid on his faithful wife. Miraculously He healed him and added twelve years to his life as only He could do.

His only sister said God called him to preach the gospel at an early age. He did not preach in a pulpit, but lived to preach over his telephone to others, including me. Sweet memories to the two of them, via a song which she sang; "There's A Leak in This Old Building My Soul Has Got to Move." Another writer penned: "Truly He Made a Difference in My Life." God does wonder working miracles in my life.

A certain man named Saul, reached from the ground. His named change to Paul with the record showing he preached from the ground asking:

"LORD, what do You want me to do?" **Acts 9:6b**.

In the process of time, one day our mission circle visited one of our deacons who was very sick at home. Upon arrival at their house, he laid resting on the couch wide awake. We exchanged greetings to him and his wife, then opened up devotion. As mission teacher at that time, I read the text in our mission book, never to forget it.

> "Therefore his sisters sent to Him saying, LORD, behold, he whom You love is sick. When Jesus heard that He said: This sickness is not unto death, but, for the glory of God that the Son of God might be glorified thereby." **John 11:3-4**.

Suddenly our deacon cried out loud with glorified God shouts of praises to Him. Immediately, he received his miracle healing. At that very moment, God healed him. Later on, he and his wife purchased a brand new home, and enjoyed God's mighty blessing together many years, miraculously in Him.

God is my witness. A second time, a well-known preacher, called to preach for Him, preached the gospel, he said fifty years or more. Obedience was his hall of fame testimony. When he took sick, I went to visit him. I talked to his wife while he sat in a wheelchair so frail, he could barely talk. Yet his wife continued to pray and spoke healing blessings over his body; asking God to heal him. She was a praying, singing evangelist in Him as well. Then it happened. One day God said, call up My preacher and say to him;

> "This sickness is not unto death." **John 11:4b**.

The preacher whispered "it is God's Word and he believed it. All I did was obeying Him."

A few days later, I ran into his wife at the marketplace, she was excited and testified that God had spoke, saying her husband would walk again. I believed her, because He said: "This sickness is not unto death."

My dear readers, when believers believe God, divine order falls in line. I ran into his wife a second time in the same marketplace. The look on her face glowed like a lamp shined within her. She had to share her testimony. Her husband's son carried him to the church he pastured, in his wheelchair. So she called to check on him. He told her he walked from his office to church that Sunday morning. I sensed her heart-felt joy. The two of us shouted gladly!

So one day I met the pastor himself in the marketplace. He praised God in the fullness of His great glory for sparing his life. He too lived years afterward. The first sermon I heard him preach was: "What Lack I Yet?" **Matthew 19:20**. In memory of the preacher who joined my husband and I together in marriage.

> "Jesus said to them, if you want to be perfect go, sale what you have and give to the poor and you will have treasure in heaven; and come, follow Me. But when the young man hears true saying he went away sorrowful, for he had great possession," **verses 21:22**.

 God is my witness that pastor revealed to me one day that he would not question my faith in God, because I discussed Sunday school lessons over our telephone without a book and it was the truth. A writer wrote a song his wife sang, titled I believe, "I'm going to take a Trip."

A glance back, our dear sweet mother was a victim of breast cancer. She passed away many years ago, but she lives within my heart. Her favorite saying to the four of us was, "mark my words". I found and pass on her mark preciously memories of a hit record. In which says "That I might know Him and the power of His resurrection and the fellowship of His sufferings being comfortable unto His death." **Philippians 3:10**.

Our mother dear walked the four of us over a mile to and from church every Sunday possible. When she was too weak to walk miles in her shoes, I discovered the church was still preciously in her heart; a secret weapon was her testimony, saying:

> "I press toward the mark for the prize of the high call of God in Christ: Let us therefore as many as be perfect have this mind: and if anything be otherwise minded, God shall reveal even this to you. Nevertheless, where to, we have already attained, let us walk by the same rule let us mind the same thing." **Vv 14-16**

Being a victim of breast cancer, when her pain grew too painful, she knew a way to escape in God.

> "For our conversation is in heaven," a taste of v 20; "Who shall change our vile body that it may be fashioned like unto His glorious body, according to the working whereby He is able even to subdue all things unto Himself." **V 21**.

Even so, I begged our dear sweet mother to wake up. When I was nearly fourteen years old, I pulled her little limp body close to my heart. But in Jesus' name, she continued to sleep on in her hall of fame resting place, famously in Him. Thinking on Paul's words I glorify God.

> "Therefore, my beloved and long for my brethren, my joy and crown so stand fast in the LORD, beloved." **4:1**.

It's a pleasure for me to spread His Word within my book, because it is a family affair. For example, Obamacare is approved by law; anyone may be insured in the land of the living. It is a joy to remain wealthily well, for he cares. Since God chose him, as He did all of His writers, Peter witnessed miracles.

> "And saw heaven opened and an object like a great sheet bound at the four corners descending to him and let down to the earth. In it were all kinds of four-footed animals of the earth, wild beasts, creeping things and birds of the air." **Acts 10:11-12**.

God captured his attention on a roof top close to heaven.

> "Then Peter went down to the men who had been sent from Cornelius, and said, Yes I am he whom you seek, for what reason have you come? And they said Cornelius, the centurion a just man one who fears God and has a good reputation among all the nation of the Jews, was divinely instructed by a holy angel to summon you to his house;" **Acts 10: 21-22a**. He needed assistance even so he; "And to hear words from you," verses **22b.**

Notably they faced Peter.

> "Then he invited them in and lodged them. On the next day Peter went away with them and some brethren from Joppa accompanied him. And the following day they entered Caesarea. Now Cornelius met him and fell down at his feet and worshipped him. But Peter lifted him up, saying, stand up; I myself am also a man," **Verses 23-26.**

Peter feared God deep within his heart.

> "And as he talked with him, he went in found many who had come together. Then he said to them, you know how unlawful it is for a Jewish man to keep company with, or to go to one of another nation. But God has shown me that I should not call any man common or unclean" **Acts 10:27-28**.

In response, to the core of my soul there is a way to smile, because Peter thought he was right, until Jesus gave him a revelation. In this shows right verses wrong. For example, as for me a witness for our LORD, I wondered why many people hate President Obama. In spite of my questions, God is infinitely influenced by power of the Spirit of obedience which pleases Him. When I gaze in my mirror, someone made in His image gazes back at me that keep me responsible for self, right verses wrong. Bowed at noon; facing the north to pray; before I could even ask Him, **Wonder**'s gathering on Memorial Day weekend flashed in my mind. This thought quickened my spirit, because I wanted to attend.

Someone called, informing me who would be attending the event from my hometown. I knew the person well. She was a young lady that used to babysit my children, and attended our school of **Wonder**. As a result, God answered and I attended the event. Long lives my joy. The strength of my life, in which great and mighty things happens in Him. And yes, the Spirit reveals all things.

> "So Cornelius said four days ago I was fasting until this hour; at the ninth hour I prayed in my house,

and behold, a man stood before me in bright clothing," **v 30**.

As far as I'm concerned, it's no secret that He reiterated joyously. I record God's blessings to him I rewrite these things saying.

> "Then Peter opened his mouth and said in truth I perceive that God shows no partiality. But in every nation whoever fears him works righteousness is accepted by Him: Which God sent to the children of Israel preaching peace through Jesus Christ He is LORD of all." **Vv 34-35.**

Overwhelmed, one very close to my heart revealed, she normally visualized her name in this particular place. But then one day instead of visualizing her name, she said saw mine. Incredible as it is, it is just a taste of Jesus' love, grace and mercies shown to me, quicker than I could flip my light switch on.

Once, there was a guest who sat at my table as I served dinner. I was speaking on God's amazing love for us. My dinner guest said in return, if God is so good, you should make two thousand dollars a week.

Instantly God breathe in my spirit:

> "The LORD is my Shepherd I shall not want."
> **Psalm 23:1**.

My guest did not say a word. For Peter said:

> "That word you know, which was proclaimed throughout all Judea, and began from Galilee after the baptism which John preached. How God

anointed Jesus of Nazareth with the Holy Spirit and
with power; who went about doing good and
healing all who was oppressed by the devil, for God
was with Him," **Acts 10:37-38**.

God is a healer for the old, young *and* outcast, as well as
for the sick, fit or unjust.

"And we are witnesses of all these things, He did
both in the land of the Jews, and in Jerusalem whom
they killed by hanging on a tree. Him God raised up
on the third day and showed Him openly, not to all
the people, but to witnesses chosen before by God
even to those who ate and drank with Him after He
arose from the dead.**" verses 39-41**. His missions
are; "He commanded us to preach, and testify that it
is He who was ordained by God to be the Judge of
the living and the dead. In Him all the prophets
witness that through His name, whosoever believes
in Him will receive remission of sins." **Verses 42-
43.**

Notably, I use God's Word:

"While Peter was still speaking these words, the
Holy Spirit fell upon all those who heard the
Word." **Verse 44**.

Cornelius was the first Gentile representative to introduce
the gospel of His grace. President Obama, the first history
making black president, God has no respect of persons.

"And those of the circumcision who believe were
astonished, as many as came with Peter, because the
Holy Spirit has been poured out of the Gentiles
also:" **Verse 45**. So, "Then Peter answered; can

> anyone forbid water, that these should be baptized who have received the Holy Spirit just as we have? And he commanded them to be baptized in the name of LORD then they asked him to stay a few days." **Verses 46b-48.**

I say again. God showed me four days before time that Mr. Obama was going to be the 44th president. And I still feel wealthily blessed in the God of all truth. So, January 20th 2009, the day Senator Obama was sworn in to office as President of the United States of America, God said to me, document every 44th verse throughout Old and New Testament. I absolutely marked every 44th verse within my Bible. I just did what God said. *Of a truth,* we ought to stand together in true unity. Since it is absolutely true, we the people of the United States voted for all white presidents these great many years. Surely we ought to think *of a truth.* God ordained the government in the first place.

Today politics remind me of the year 1992. I believe, Washington D.C. hosted a workshop and the staff on Aging attended, while we were employed at East Central Arkansas EDC. The workshop was titled, *The Dirtiness of Politics*, in likeness of today's dirty politics. A couple of 60+ senior citizens also attended, to understand the program in action. But one thing we learned, our Congressman, from Arkansas at that time, demonstrated his concern for seniors, because of his dear mom. We had much respect for him. He made sure seniors received what was needful for ECA Aging. He even took group pictures with us there in D.C. that made us feel wealthy. Race did not seem to matter to him. In my opinion, he was a very fair congressman. I wish the materials we used in those four or five days were on file today, so I could have shared a taste of the results.

I remember a precious blessing that we were able to ride on the Spirit of Washington to see the bridge open up. It was a beautiful sight to see. But a storm caught us out on the river with the wind blowing, lightning flashing and thunder rolling. The rain continuously poured down before we could return to land. We made it back safely though. I was afraid, because I had a bad experience on a lake once, with a few of my classmates when we were attending **Wonder**. We almost drown, but God was present to prevent that from happening, just as He was that day in D.C.

> "And when they saw Him walking on the sea they supposed it was a ghost cried out, for all saw Him, and were troubled. But immediately He talked to them and said be of good cheer; it is I be not afraid: Then he went to them up into the boat to them, and the wind ceased." **Mark 6:49-51a**.

Because of Him, great things happened.

> "And they were greatly amazed in themselves beyond measure, and marveled. For they had not understood about the, loathes, because their hearts were hardened," **Verse 51b**.

See the amazing announcement. Many people who touched Him were made well. David's prayers of confidence, written to all, shall not be forgotten.

> "Preserve me, O God, for in You I put my trust. O my soul, you have said to the LORD, You are my LORD, My goodness is nothing apart from You. As

for the saints who are on the earth, they are the excellent ones, in who is my delight." **Psalm 16:1-3**.

Delighted, I received God's excellent blessings with a warning to all generations saying:

"Their sorrows shall be multiplied who hasten after other gods; their drink offerings of blood I will not offer, nor take up their names on my lips." **Verse 4**.

God made a way for His servant to escape a hard core spirit, if ever there was a man who offered praises to God, it was David. He was hand-picked. Likewise, I delight myself diligently in Him.

"O LORD, You are the potion of my inheritance and my cup; You maintain my lot: The lines have fallen to me in pleasant places; yes I have a good inheritance I will bless the LORD who has given me counsel my heart also instructs me in the night season." Verses **5-7**; David increased his revelations in addition, by saying.

"I have set the LORD always before me; because He is at my right hand I shall not be moved: Therefore my heart is glad my glory rejoices; my flesh will rest in hope" **verse 9**.

An old and famous song revealed the above Scripture, titled, "I Shall Not Be Moved."

Clearly as the Son of God is our Savior, he knew his LORD, and said:

"For You will not leave my soul in hell, nor will you allow Your Holy One see corruption. You will show the path of life; in your presence is fullness of joy at Your right hand are pleasures forevermore." **Verses 10-11**

Shareholders by faith are partakers as was David. He did not flip flop when he said:

"Hear a just cause, attend to my cry; give ear to my prayer, which is not from deceitful lips. Let your vindication come from Your presence; let Your eyes look on the things that are upright. You have tested my heart: You have visited me in the night: You have tried me and have found nothing." **Psalm 17:1-3a**.

Midnight they say is the darkest hour of night. Ruth obeyed Naomi at midnight, and David who was in the family said.

"I have purposed that my mouth shall not transgress: Concerning the works of men by the word of Your lips, I have kept away from the paths of the destroyer. Uphold my steps in Your paths that my footsteps may not slip. I have called upon You, for You will hear me, O God: incline Your ear to me, and hear my speech." **Verses 3b-6**

A writer recorded song titled, "Up Hold Me LORD,"

David penned:

"Show Your marvelous loving-kindness by Your right hand. O You who saves them who trust in You from those who rise up against them. Keep me as the apple of your eye; Hide me under the shadow of your wings." **Verses 7a-8**

Two young men appeared to be, 'slipping into darkness', but God always has a purpose planned. The two of them were in court for failure to pay child support. They looked like children who wake up in the darkest hour afraid; looking for their daddy. One sat next to me. Boldly I asked him, who is highest after God? He replied the devil. The one who sat next to him laughed out loud at him. Then he explained how alcohol was a bad habitually practice for him. He continued to explain that had it not been for alcohol he would be a good man. Then I confessed, during my younger years, I drank and enjoyed parties with friends. But I had to give up clubs and party at home, because babysitter fees were no laughing matter, even during those good old days.

Being a witnessed for God, it was a natural thing for me to speak boldly to them, which was a message from above. I was there because someone asked me to give them a ride to court. Then I encouraged the two young men by saying, God loves us beyond alcohol, drugs, faults and habits. When we ask Jesus to help us, He will aid us.

Then it happened. I purposely left the two of them on the edge of their seats needing to hear more of God. Remembering God blessed David, whether he was in a pit, among his enemies, or hidden from Saul. David said:

> "As for me, I will see Your face in righteousness; I shall be satisfied when I wake up in Your likeness."
> **Verse 15**.

I say again. Awake or asleep, God is always right. A friend and former classmate of **Wonder** always said the two of us gained a natural high in Him, after we learned to lay aside things too difficult for us.

I have sweet memory of my friend, God rest her soul, because she said God would not allow her to stay here and suffer much longer and she was absolutely right. He called her name the day I had to revisit **Psalms 25:1-22,** in which her sweet family recorded in her eulogy.

I dreamt I was in a deep dark tunnel under ground. A light shined deep in the pit. I said to my decease husband Joe, but called him Paul, and shared my dream with him. He shook his head side to side and told me not to worry; he was all right with God. I believed him with a sweet memory of **Acts 9**. God used Paul. It was Joe's body in my dream, but it was my only son's voice that spoke to me.

God woke me up safe in my bed, but He revealed a double revelation. A reminder of our sweet mother, speechless at times, for her pain was great. When she returned to the hospital, we were not allowed to visit her ward. But our grand's found a place for us to wave to her from the ground. We couldn't hear her voice, but we could see her smiling face. This brings to mind an old Doctor Watt the elders still sing today; "If I couldn't say a word, I would just wave my hand."

A friend and I attended a three day revival where a preacher preached glimpses of Peter's sermon, saying:

> "And they continued steadfastly in the apostle's doctrine and fellowship in the breaking of bread and in prayers. Then fear came up on every soul and

many signs and wonders were done through the apostles. Now all who believes were together and had all things in common. And sold their possessions, goods divided them among all." **Acts 2:42-45a**

Reality clicked in; revealing great things:

"As anyone had need they continuing daily with one accord in the temple breaking bread from house to house, they ate their food with gladness and simplicity of heart. Praising God and having favor with all people: And the LORD added to the church daily such as should be saved," **verses 45b-47**.

Chapter Four
"The Results"
1st of Four Books

Imagine praising and worshiping God in a raging storm that goes on and on thirty-eight long years then on a sunshiny day with a clear blue sky. It's not imaginary.

> "Now Peter and John went up together to the temple at the hour of prayer, the ninth hour: And a certain man lame from his mothers' womb was carried whom they laid daily at the gate of the temple that is called Beautiful to ask alms from those who entered the temple; who seeing Peter and John about to go in the temple asked alms." **Acts 3:1-3**.

A nameless, lame man expected help:

> "And fixing his eyes on him with John; Peter said, look on us: So he gave them his attention expecting to receive something from them; Then Peter said, Silver and gold I do not have, but what I do have I give you: In the name of Jesus Christ of Nazareth rise up and walk." **Verses 4-6**

Influenced by the power of God they,

> "Took him by the right hand and lifted him up, and immediately his ankle bones received strength: "So he leaping up, stood and walked and entered the temple with them walking and leaping and praising God." **verses 7-8**.

My dear readers, I'm reminded of the pastor within my first chapter whom I met in the marketplace. He always said, "I've never done better in my life." In specialized memory of him, I've never forgotten the old pastor's words he spoke those many years ago. As result, miracles happened even beyond the new pastor's desires, which God sent to pastor that church. He desired to see miracles and they happened. But that's not his own true story, because Jesus worked it out for him. I share with my family and whosoever will listen. I love spreading great news. If it's good news about God, I will tell it.

For instance, Monday night jail ministry with a woman of faith was special times in the midst, as we ministered to women who welcomed God's Word. Yet in the process of time, other women of faith desired to minister in that place. But later it was revealed to us, there were too many arriving to witness to the ladies.

 So I moved on, as God made room for others to enjoy witnessing for Him, in that famed hall of notoriety that humbled someone like me for life. Then Saturday evening a husband and wife held specialized prayer services at 4:00 p.m. for many years. I was in the midst of prayer when a certain church closed down. After the church closed, the couple invited us to their home to keep on praying. God made room for us in there.

I especially remember them being like two love birds. She always joked with us by saying, had we not continued praying at their home, they would have split up. It was an absolute joy hanging with these elders. In remembering that, I'm reminded of a young lady who practiced a song; "I

Would Rather Have JESUS Than Silver And Gold.
Distinctively it is written saying:

> "And all the people saw him walking and praising
> God. Then they knew that it was he who sat
> begging alms at the Beautiful Gate of the temple:
> And they were filled with wonder and amazement at
> what had happened to him." **Acts 3:9-10.**

There are words a good friend said to me, during her
lifetime on earth, are celebrated and cherished. Words, I
say, helped her to understand. We take our physical bodies
to physicians for checkups. Likewise, we should ask our
God for spiritual healing and cleansing that is to instill in us
the real church begins *in* us within our spirit by His Spirit.
For the cause it is written.

> "But those things which God foretold by the mouth
> of His prophets, that the Christ would suffer; He has
> thus fulfilled." V 18, "God has spoken by the mouth
> of all His holy prophets since the world began;"
> **Acts 3:21b.**

 Even far as His heavens are above, after all said and done,
God's proposes and mighty plans work. President Obama
and Vice President Biden's days within the Whitehouse are
approved by God and the majority of the citizens also.

My younger sister, her son and I were on a three way
conference call together. Suddenly, my nephew, who is a
preacher of the gospel, said he thought he was pretty good
preaching history lessons.   That is until he heard and
listened to President Obama spoke on it notably. In respect
to my nephew's humility, in favor of his remarks, as for me

also, our president is a man I respect abundantly. A writer wrote a song titled I believe is absolutely true. "God Never Fails."

> "For Moses truly said to the fathers, The LORD your God will raise up for you a Prophet like me for your brethren. Him you will hear in all things whatever He says to you. And it shall be that every soul who will not hear that Prophet shall be utterly destroyed from among the people." **Verse e22-23**.

Then it happened. We, and whosoever believes in this place and follow our God, are included.

> "Yes and all the prophets from Samuel and those who follow, as many as have spoken, have also foretold these days. You are sons of the prophets, and of the covenant which God made with our fathers, saying to Abraham, and in your seed all the families of the earth shall be blessed." **V 25**

We are in this place as recorded:

> "To you first, God having raised up His Servant Jesus sent Him to bless You, in turning away every one of you from your iniquities." **V 26**

The palmist shares great blessings, in which I am so glad to invest in the evidence always, says.

> "For the LORD is a sun and shield; the LORD will give grace and glory; no good will He withhold from those who walk uprightly. O LORD of hosts, blessed is the man who trusts in You." **Psalm 84:11-12**,

One Sunday afternoon the witness team was delightedly
set up to share God's Word. Suddenly a lady that stayed in
the area strolled over and said to us, "hey I want some of
what you people have." We welcomed her to pray with us
positively, because she refreshed my spirit, especially since
we used to party together in our young adult years.
Genuinely, I know God's doors are opened He allows
anyone to come right in saved, unsaved and willing to be
saved are genuinely invited to enter into His gates. As a
result, I love to tell the true story, although I'm guilty as
charged. But God's love, grace and mercies saved a wretch
like me for life, by His amazing affirmative action plan
through Jesus Christ our Savior I trust Him. The psalmist
report says:

> "Rejoice in the LORD, O you righteous! For praise
> from the upright is beautiful. Praise the LORD with
> the harp; Make melody to Him with an instrument
> on ten strings. Sing to Him a new song; Play
> skillfully with a shout For the Word of the LORD is
> right and His work is done in truth," **Psalm 33:1-4**.

Once, an elder deacon sang a song, titled, "Never Grow
Old". I believe the writer would have rejoiced, had he heard
him imitate him. In remembering the deacon, the song
seemed to fit his shoe size, because he rejoiced in God
saying.

> "He loves righteousness and justice; the earth is full
> of the goodness of the LORD, By the Word of the
> LORD the heavens were made and all the host of
> them by the breath of His mouth. He gathers the
> water of the sea together as a heap; He lays up the

deep in the storehouses." **Verses 5-7**, effectively: "Let all the earth fear the LORD; Let all the inhabitants of the world stand in awe of Him: He spoke, and it was done; He commanded, and it stood fast. The LORD brings the counsel of the nations to nothing; He makes the plans of the peoples of no effect." **Verses 8-10**

The writer understood His Maker above all things and recorded these words from the heart:

> "The counsel of the LORD stands forever, the plans of His heart to all generations. Blessed is the nation whose God is the LORD, the people He has chosen as His own inheritance. The LORD looks from heaven; and sees all men: From the place of His dwelling He looks on all inhabitances of the earth," **verses 11-14**.

A writer penned a hymnal, titled "Blessed Assurance." A former student of my older sister of our school **Wonder** leads the song often. She shared with me a few years ago in morning service. we were elders of the church, due to the facts our mothers had passed away before they reached our ages. In precious memories of our mothers, may they rest in peace; and may God continue to use us anyway He desires to. It is alright with me. The psalmist made it plain, I believe, in honor to them . God:

> "Fashions their hearts individually He considers all their works: No man is saved by a multitude of an army; a mighty man is not delivered by great strength." **Verses 15-16**, God called to my attention

to His Word says. "A horse is a vain hope for safety; neither shall it deliver by its great strength. Behold, the eye of the LORD is on those who fear Him" verses **17-18a**.

In special memory of a precious teenager who in his life, looked excellent on horseback, I believe, in the eyes of God. It is an honor to make mention of him in my God breathe book watched by many on T.V. screens across the country and beyond. Yet God keeps their amazing parents, families, friends and whosoever endures such. He sent special help to them to pray one day at a time for them. Preciously, and we should remember all young people killed in action across the world in vain; those we know and do not know about, but God sees all things.

A special young boy, loved by his family, was killed like a wild beast died instantly. As results a few preachers, pastors and community volunteers organized a team to help our young people in our hometown God in the midst, I joined them. However, we must follow before becoming a leader. Someone in an action agency asked me to humanize the young boy in a closed door meeting, a place for justice for God's children whether believers or unbelievers, because He is our Justifier.

Good Samaritans volunteers, a few in numbers included me worked two years within a neighbor church. We met once a week determined to make a difference within our city. Since we had a taste of good times learning to work together the psalmist said:

"On hope in His mercy; **Psalm 33:18b**.

In Him our hope lingers on; houses for homeless; sight to the blind; insight to agree.

> "Our soul waits for the LORD; He is our help, and shield. For our heart shall rejoice in Him, Because we have trusted in His holy name, Let Your mercy, O LORD, be upon us, Just as we hope in You."
> **Verses 20-22**

Trusting God our Creator, Jesus our Savior, the Holy Spirit our Helper is always present even in our down time, as it is written:

> "The next day John saw Jesus coming to him, and said, Behold! The Lamb of God who takes the sin of the world! This is He of whom I said, after me comes a Man who is preferred before me, for He was before me." **John 1:29-30**.

God sent a Word today, even when sin is on the rampage. John revealed:

> "I did not know Him, but that He should be revealed to Israel, therefore I came baptizing with water. And John bore witness, saying I saw the Spirit descending from heaven like a dove, and he remained on Him." **Verses 31-32**

A song writer wrote "This Little Light of Mine I'M Going to Let it Shine," so let it shine.

I was riding down with a group, to participate in a prison ministry miles from home. It was a beautiful day and the group rejoiced faithfully; talking about Jesus all the way.

When we arrived at the site, a young man on the back seat we thought was asleep, suddenly he shouted out: when you hurt too much to pray, just say Jesus three times! We didn't say a word. As for me, I've been in that place many times. Fitting in with the young man's words, a song came to mind; "Jesus, Jesus, Jesus." So I fill in with my own words.

I was so amazed. I saw two young men from our hometown, in which I met walking the streets witnessing Christ within our hometown, West Memphis Arkansas. The trip was a very good treat, especially since the young men, and I remembered each other. 'Looking to Jesus,' we read scriptures, prayed, and sang praises to God abundantly, before closing out in prayer. I said to myself, Jail house ministry rock in Him when men join together awesomely lifting up Jesus in the place. Remembering, a thought inspired me; especially when women prisoners sang together. It was indeed a pleasure to be locked up in the same cell with them to share His Word. For instance, the women could really pray and sing a song titled, I believe, "Way Down Yonder All By Myself, I Couldn't Hear Nobody Pray." As a result, church begins in us anytime, anyplace and I am a witness praising God. I got a message from the LORD, it is the way He uses people; "The way to escape" insanity.

> "Thus says the LORD to His anointed, to Cyrus, whose right hand I have held. To subdue nations before him and loose the arms of kings, to open before him the double doors, so that the gates will not be shut: I will go before you; and make the crooked place straight. I will break in pieces the

gates of bronze and cut the bars of iron," **Isaiah 45:1-2**.

God is our source, as He promised us saying:

> "I will give you the treasures of darkness and hidden riches of secret places: That you may know that I, the LORD, Who called you by your name, I Am the God of Israel." **Verse 3 see 4-25! Glancing at Jesus and all that happened at a glimpse says.**

> "He went through every city and village, preaching and bringing glad tidings of the kingdom of God. And the twelve were with Him, and a certain woman who had been healed of evil spirits and infirmities, Mary called Magdalene, out of whom had come seven demons," **Luke 8:1b-2**.

Miraculously, Mary was not alone it is recorded for us to know the way to work together say.

> "Joanna, the wife of Chuza, Herod's steward, and Susanna and many others who provided for Him from their substance, and when a great multitude had gathered and they had come to Him from every city He spoke a parable;" Verses **3-4**.

So it is true, if we follow Jesus. The test on earth began in action, but we must keep our minds on Him and examine these things saying.

> "A sower went out to sow his seed and as he sowed some fell by the wayside; and it trampled down and the birds of the air devoured it." **Verse 5**

And it is no secret to believers or unbelievers.

"But others fell on good ground, sprang up, and yielded a crop, a hundredfold. When He had said these things He cried out, He who has ears to hear let him hear!" **Verse 8**.

To my amazement, it happened to me. Trusting God causes people to watch our character; the way we act, even at church. A young pastor, an apostle of God, stood up, prayed and took his text early one Sunday morning and read:

"Now on the first day of the week Mary Magdalene went to the tomb early, while it was still dark, and saw that the stone had been taken away from the tomb. Then she ran and came to Simon Peter; and the other disciple whom Jesus loved said to them: They have taken away the LORD out of the tomb, we do not know where they have laid Him:" **John 20: I-2.**

The young pastor said God told him to preach the message in honor to me, yours truly. He said, she is always on time for early services every Sunday. Flabbergasted, I asked a mother of the church what did he say? She confirmed his words.

Once Mary Magdalene met Jesus, her life changed, as did mine. We named our mission circle in memory of her. I ordered tee shirts; paid for them with her name printed on them. The same woman Jesus made a way for her to escape seven devils, because He had need of her works, by faith in Him; same as me. An elderly lady prayed for missionaries and God answered her prayers. Four women attended the Monday night gathering, included me. She was the mother of a former classmate of our older sister. We were elders in the church; for our moms had passed away at our ages; she sang "Blessed Assurance", in memory of our mothers. God blessed them. Her mom lived for years after our mom passed. And yet before she passed, she spoke a message from the LORD saying, read your Bible before studying my commentary!

> "But Mary stood outside by the tomb weeping; as she wept she stooped down and looked within the tomb. And she saw two angels in white sitting, one at the head and the other at the feet where the body of Jesus had lain. Then they said to her, Woman, why, are you weeping? She said to them, because they have taken away my LORD" **John 20:11-13a**

She had an early morning assignment saying,

> "I do not know where they laid Him. Now when she had said this, she turned around and saw Jesus standing there and she did not know it was Jesus. Jesus said to her woman why are you weeping? Whom are you seeking? Verses 13b-15a

It is a true saying; early we seek God, early we find Him. I'm delighted He knows our names.

> "And she, supposing Him to be the gardener, said to Him, Sir if You have carried Him away, tell me where You have laid Him, and I will take Him away. Jesus said to her, Mary! She turned and said to Him, Rabboni! Which is to say Teacher" **verses 15b-16**

In Him, love hope and charity revealed.

"Jesus said to her do not cling to Me! For I have not yet ascended to My Father, but go to My brethren say to them, I Am ascending to My Father and My God and your God. Mary Magdalene came and told the disciples that she had seen the LORD, and that He has spoken these things to her." **Verses 17-18 see 20-31.**

Indeed, it's a family affair; Father, Son, and Holy Spirit.

For instance, it was revealed my twin brother and I kicked together in our mother's womb. Amazingly we were born on her birthday. Imagine our dad and mom cooed over me then an hour later my twin was borne; was not imaginary. They said we were sprinkled as babies, for our dad was a Methodist pastor who passed away.

Years later, we sat on the mourner's bench; confessed and accepted Jesus as Savior. I was baptized at eleven years old at Beautiful Zion Baptist church; the place papa attended. My twin brother was baptized at First Baptist. The same church my membership is on record today. God spoke and told me to go to First Baptist years ago. I obey Him and didn't keep it to self. God is my witness, same as others. Our brother graduated from **Wonder**. He married; had kids and worked in a factory. Later he moved to a big city; the same place our two uncles lived for years.

After he attended and completed a trade, he was gainfully employed. He took care of his family. I never knew why, nor my sisters, but after years working in that big city, on May 1983, my twin brother shot himself. They said before he passed, he asked God to forgive him. Before he died, he shared with me over the phone that God had called him to preach the gospel. I believed him. He asked God if He wanted him to preach on a cold cloudy Sunday in November, with the sun breaking through his bedroom window. The second time he asked God, if He wanted him to preach, to show it to his right hand. It happened and he properly read:

> "And there was a man whose right hand was withered." **Luke 6:6-11**.

This scripture revealed something happening to his right hand, same as his.

I never judged him. God is Judge. We loved him just as he was. My brother wanted to sing like Wilson Picket. Before he passed, he sent his favorite album titled. "The LORD Will Make Away Somehow." But I wasn't there when he died neither were my sisters. But he confessed before he passed over telephone lines. The metric system had gotten the best of him. The last time he returned to our hometown, a Methodist pastor allowed him to purchase communion at the church we attended. The same church we attended with our dear sweet mother, during her life time many years ago. But we do know he never did get over her death, or the way pain wracked through her body. Being her only son, our only brother suffered abundantly. I could go on about our lives in those days. Love and happiness continues as written.

> "Now it came to pass in those days that He went out to the mountain to pray, and continued all night in prayer to God. And when it was day, He called His disciples to Himself; and from then He chose twelve whom he named apostles," **Luke 6:12-13**

All I know for sure; He called my name too, and said, "I want you to be my sanctified witness. And I continue to witness for Him, so be it.

Our only brother showed me the way cigarettes harmed smokers years ago by blowing smoke into a white handkerchief. This revealed the staining color of tobacco. A writer once wrote, "Someone is trying to tell us Something Good." Cigarettes were harmful, yet I smoked anyway.

But early one Friday morning, the power came over me I could not get a cigarette between my lips. It was awesome results from Him. I've been smoke free for years. But first I had to tear up the cigarettes. I was sick and tired them! God helped me; it was Him! His doctor Luke said believe in Him: "And the power of the LORD was present to heal them," **Luke 5:17b**.

In bitter sweet, notable memories, my twin, our brother and mother are gone. The three of us are left alive by God's precious grace. A writer wrote our thoughts, I believe in the words saying; "I know He Lives within our Heart," My brother was a husband; the father of five children. As for me, I'm sticking to my own testimony; I believe these things express who we are saying.

> "You arc of God, little children and you have overcome them, because He who is in you is greater than he who is in the world." **1st John 4:4**.

 I invested in a song I listen to today titled; "I Put It All In His Hand, Big This, Big That, Little This, And Little That in His Hand"

Years ago a precious family member and the choir from Detroit were invited to celebrate Jesus journeyed to

Nashville TN. Before the choir sang, the minister of music asked anyone to hold hands make a circle and volunteer to open up in prayer. I was highly inspired, because they had traveled so far by faith in our God. I accepted the invitation to pray a bit of fear within, inspired, "For God has not given us the spirit of fear, but of power, and love, and a sound mind" **2nd Timothy 1:7**.

A few months ago, my telephone rang. Someone very close said come pray with me. Oil in hand, I went and prayed. I anointed the infected place; opened my Bible and read:

> "Saying touch not My anointed ones and do My prophets no harm," **Psalm 105:14**.

 In God, I anointed the man, his wife and myself. I put it all in His hands then headed home. God confirmed his healing just as a train approached a guarded crossing. I opened my Bible housed in my truck for times as these. My eyes fell on **Isaiah 38th Chapter**. I believed God healed him at that moment, as it is recorded in awe:

> "In those days Hezekiah was sick unto death. And Isaiah the prophet, the son of Amos went to see him and said to him: Thus said the LORD: Set your house in order: For you shall die and not live. Then Hezekiah turned his face toward the wall, and prayed to the LORD." **38:1-2**, sincerely there are great verses I rewrite; "And said, remember now, O LORD, I pray, how I have walked before You in truth and with a loyal heart and have done what is good in Your sight. And Hezekiah wept bitterly. And the word of the LORD came to Isaiah saying,

Go tell Hezekiah, thus says the LORD, the God of David your father: I have heard your prayer."
Verses 3-5a:

Then God made a promised saying,

> "Surely I will add to your days fifteen years. I will deliver you and this city from the hand of king of Assyria and I will defend this city," **verse 5**.

I said to my soul in wonder, it was a done deal. The king was healed. The word was out. It reminds me. I never denied God; I know He is Healer. I looked up at the sky in my midnight hour; God's little star in likeness, looked like it twinkled back at me. A young lady sang in which I could barely hold my peace, within a nursing home ministry. She sang, "LORD Make Me Real." Yes, He is real a writer said,

> "And this is a sign to you from the LORD that you will do this thing which He has spoken. Behold, I will bring the shadow on the sundial, which has gone down with the sun on the sundial of Ahaz ten degrees backward: So the sun returned ten degrees on the dial by which it had gone down" **verses 7-8**.

I remember a wise elder in our Sunday school class said, had she not read,

> "Joshua spoke to the LORD in the day when the LORD delivered up the Amorites before the children of Israel, and He said in the sight of Israel Sun, stand still over Gibeon; and the Moon in the valley of Aijalon so the sun stool still, and the moon

stopped till the people had revenge upon their enemies," **Joshua 10:12-13**.

God showed His servants Joshua and Hezekiah. This includes those of us who are chosen to know there is nothing too hard for God, saying.

> "The writing of Hezekiah king of Judah, when he had been sick and recovered from his sickness;" **Isaiah 38:9a**.

Years ago, God said turn your face to the wall; pray for healing. Obediently I faced my north wall. My doctor's office called to tell me to come in for a recheck. God healed me. I believed Him. These great words hang on my south wall, as it is written until this day.

> "O LORD, by these things men live. And in all these things is the life of my spirit;" **Isaiah 38:16**.

God's amazing healing blessings work. He ordered my steps. Later that week my test results were okay. I stuck to my belief.

A pit, a grave and the amazing lump of figs were God's orders to His king. Then it happened; maybe at midnight or before daylight.

> "For Isaiah said, let them take a lump of figs and apply it as a poultice on the boil and he shall recover. And Hezekiah had said, what is the sign I shall go up to the house of the LORD?" **Verse 22**

Once, one of my **Wonder** classmates was in a trance at the point of death. While I talked on my telephone, another of our class mates had visited her in the hospital intensive care unit. She said her friend was not going to live. I did not visit her in the hospital, but said boldly, God said she is not going to die. I saw that morning, and stuck to His amazing **38th chapter**. He healed her from the top of her head to the bottom of her two feet.

Years later, she's still alive and doing fine. And I have to confess; her husband believed God, because we agreed He was going to heal her. I retold her true story and revealed to her the amazing true story written within the Bible years ago. My belief in Him provided relief revealed to someone like me. What, where, when, why and how do I escape to His marvelously plan of safely. Jesus sent an invitation to all people, as it is written below.

> "Come to Me, all you who labor and are heavy laden, and I will give you rest. Take my yoke upon you and learn of Me: For I AM gentle and lowly in heart, and you will find rest for your souls. For My yoke is easy and My burden is light." **Mathew 11:28-30**.

I was standing in my kitchen, one day when God spoke the above words. I begin to rest in Him, because I'm almost at the last words of this book. His load gets heavy; leaning and learning a taste of more. My next book will be lighter, for I stick to His blessings. I got so sick after my God given revelation, I could barely think straight. He spoke the right words to me. I'm one of many, when things are better, or worst. God has first and last words and all in between. I absolutely pray and rest in Him.

In my opinion the psalmist recorded eloquently for all the days of our lives in the presence of God. For instance, President Obama and Vice President Biden are two blessed men, willing to work for all people within the United States of America.

> "Blessed is the man who walks not in the counsel of the ungodly, nor stands in the path of sinners, nor sits in the seat of the scornful; But his delight is in the law of the LORD and he meditates day and night: He shall be like a tree planted by the rivers of water that brings forth its fruit in its season whose leaf also shall not wither" **Psalm 1:1-3a**

Absolutely nothing is more wonderful than to pass on the results.

> "And whatever he does shall prosper," **verse 3b**:

It is well known to us two-ways, to live on His earth with choices every day. But,

> "The ungodly art not so, But they are like the chaff which the wind drives away. Therefore the ungodly shall not stand in judgment: Nor sinners in the congregation of the righteous: For the LORD knows the way of the righteous. But the way of the ungodly shall perish," **Verse 6**.

A young lady was burdened down with heavy weights. But then God planted a seed of faith, and it began to grow a song written, "Though, the Load Gets heavy, You're Never Left Alone At All." Luke declared:

> 'When he saw Jesus, he cried out and fell down before him, and with a loud voice said, what have I

to do with You, Jesus Son of the Most High God? I beg You do not torment me!" **Luke 8:28**.

Beware! A way to escape demon spirits reveals they have families; extended family; and friends; as does believers, for many unbelievers met Jesus.

> "For He commanded the unclean spirit to come out of the man: For it has often seized him, and he was kept under guard bound with chains and shackles and he broke the bonds and was driven by the demon into the wilderness. Jesus asked him his name? And he said Legion, because many demons had entered him." **Verses 29-30**

The young lady listened for Jesus' warns us the way demons work says:

> "And they begged Him that He would not command them to go out into the deep. Now a herd of many swine was feeding there on the mountain. So they begged Him that He would permit them to enter them: And He permitted them." **Verses 31-32**

Amazing thoughts crept in my spirit.

> "Then the demons went out of the man and entered the swine, and the herd ran down violently down the steep place into the lake and drowned. When those who fed them saw what happened, they fled and told it in the city and in the country." **Luke 8:33-34**.

Aware of what happened at the site, Jesus knew what was next in line.

> "Then they went out to see what had happened, and
> came to Jesus and found the man from whom the
> demons had departed, sitting at the feet of Jesus
> clothed in his right mind. And they were afraid.
> They also who had seen it told them by what means
> he who had been demon-possessed was healed."
> **Verses 35-36 See 37-42.**

A song writer wrote, "It is good to Know Jesus," mindfully
demons enter in without invitations yet demon was set free.
When one obeyed Jesus and went running back to his
hometown to tell his true story, delightedly clothed in his
right mind. For instance, when a good sale goes on in the
marketplaces, whether food, clothes, shoes, etc., Good
Samarians work for Jesus every day says.

> "Now a woman, having a flow of blood for twelve
> years, who had spent all her livelihood on
> physicians and could not be healed by any, came
> from behind and touched the hem of His garment.
> And immediately her flow of blood stopped:"
> **Verses 43-44**.

 A writer wrote double blessings. I fell in love with a song
that's titled. "Yes it is Jesus, Wonderful Jesus, because, I
touched the hem of His garment and His love made me
whole."

Luke wrote:

> "And Jesus said, who touched Me? When all denied
> it, Peter and those with him said, Master, the
> multitudes throng and press You and You say Who
> touched Me? Again, "Jesus said somebody touched

Me for I perceive power going out from Me."
Verses 45-46

A family member had problems. As we discussed them, I said to her that's life on earth, so be it. And she answered back that's right!

> "Now when the woman saw that she was not hidden, she came trembling; and falling down before Him, she declared to Him in the presence of all the people, the reason she had touched Him and how she was healed immediately. And He said to her: Daughter, be of good cheer; your faith had made you well: Go in peace," **verses 47-48** see **vv 49-55**. "And her parents were astonished, but He charged them to tell no one what had happened;" **Verse 56.**

I'm determined to remain encouraged, even when the birthers constantly report to the media President Obama lacks a birth certificate. They claim he wasn't born in the United States of America. I stay encouraged in Him. The next day I received a copy of our president's birth certificate in the mail. It was certainly remarkably. For the Democrats proof, revealed the state of Hawaii, file 151 Department of Health 61 1064, as others were unremarkable. Mr. Obama and Mr. Biden absolutely serve in the right place.

But we never heard of birthers or tea party haters when we voted for white presidents. I believe David did when he wrote this Psalm acknowledging these things saying.

> "The LORD is my light and my salvation, who shall
> I fear; the LORD is the strength of my life; of
> whom shall I be afraid? When the wicked, even,
> my enemies; and my foes came up against me to eat
> up my flesh they stumbled and fell." **Psalm 27:1-2**

God is a good Master over my life, and I pass on praises of
prayer in Him that kept us safe; **see verses 3-14.**

Our grand's kept us well asafetida bags which I hated
because they smelled bad. Yet we had to wear them on our
necks. Anyway, we prayed for presidents in the White
House who held the highest position under God in
America. Rethinking, the President and Vice President
perform great works.

> "When Jesus departed from there, two blind men
> followed Him, crying out and saying, Son of David,
> have mercy on us! And when He had come into the
> house, the blind came to Him. And Jesus said to
> them, do you believe that I am able to do this? They
> said to Him, Yes LORD." **Matthew 9:27-28.**
> Justice works in Him. "Then He touched their eyes
> saying, according to your faith let it be to you. And
> their eyes were open:" **Verse 29-30.**

There is a song famously titled with high ratings in Him on
earth; "Only Believe", and I do.

> "But when they had departed, they spread the news
> about Him in all that country. As they went out,
> they brought to Him a man, mute and demon-

possessed: And when the demon was cast out, the mute spoke. And the multitude marveled, saying, it was never seen like this in Israel!" **verses 31-33**. "The Pharisees said, He casts out demons by the ruler of the demons," **verse 34**.

Did they not know there is nothing too hard for God? Moving forward there is a Word from above;

"Then Jesus went about all the cities and villages teaching in their synagogues, preaching the gospel of the kingdoms and healing every sickness and every disease among the people:" **verse 35.** But it wasn't over yet. He looked, "But when He saw the multitudes He was moved with compassion for then, because they were weary and scattered, like having no shepherd. Then He said to His disciples: The labors are few, Therefore pray the LORD of harvest to send out laborers into the harvest," **Verses 36-38**.

Jesus left His mark on His disciples; a way to escape being blind in Him.

"Then it happened, as He was coming near Jericho, when a certain blind man sat by the road begging. And hearing a multitude passing by, he asked what it meant. So they told him that Jesus of Nazareth was passing by: And he cried out saying, Jesus, Son of David, have mercy of me!" **Luke 18:35-38**.

A blind man heard Jesus approaching, but his name isn't on record, but God knew him!

"Then those who went before warned him that he should be quite; But, he cried out all the more, Son of David, have mercy on me. So Jesus stood still and commanded him to be brought to Him saying, "What do you want Me to do for you? He said LORD that I may receive my sight." **Verses 39-41** One thing is clear to us preciously, "Then Jesus said to him, receive your sight: your faith has made you well. And immediately he received his sight and followed Him, glorifying God: And all the people, when they saw it and gave praise to God." **Verses 42-43**

Imagine a song; "I Once Was Blind but Now I see." I sang, "God has smiled on me"; eye openers are God given wisdom working wonders. He knows our names.

For instance,

"Now two women who were harlots came to the king, and stood before him. One woman said, O my lord this woman and I dwell in the same house; and I gave birth while she was in the house. Then it happened, the third day after I had given birth that this woman also gave birth. And we were together;" **1st Kings 3:16-18a**.

One was right, one was wrong; one confessed.

"No one was with us in the house, except the two of us. And this woman's son died in the night;" **verses 18b-19**.

It could have midnight, because it was at night.

"So she arose in the middle of the night and took my son from my side while your maidservant slept and laid him in her bosom." **Verses 20: see v 23**.

Amazingly, God chose a wise king who knew how to crack a nut.

"Then the king said, bring me a sword. And the king said, divide the living child in two, and give half to one, and the half to the other. Then the woman whose son was living spoke to the king, for she yearned with compassion for her son, and said O lord, give her the living child by no means kill him," **verses 24-26 see 28a**. "And they feared the king, for they saw that the wisdom of God was with him to administer justice."**V 28b.**

"Then Jesus entered and passed through Jericho. Now behold, there was a man named Zacchaeus who was a chief tax collector and he was very rich. And he sought to see who He was; but he could not see who Jesus was; and could not for the press because he was little of stature." **Luke 19:1-3**.

The little man had to meet Jesus that same day:

"And he ran before, and climbed up in a sycamore tree to see Him, for He was going to pass his way." **Verse 4**.

Amazingly and purposely Jesus had plans of His own.

"And when Jesus came to the place, He looked up and saw him and said to him Zacchaeus, make haste and come down, for today I must stay at your house: So he made haste and came down, and received Him joyfully." **Verses 5-6**

The chief tax collector was accepted an invitation planned that certain day and hour;

> "But when they saw it, they all complained, saying, He has gone to be guest with a man that is a sinner." **Verse 7**.

That didn't hinder Jesus, because the results show; looking up to Him.

> "Zacchaeus stood and said to the LORD, Look, LORD, I give half of my goods to the poor and if I have taken anything from anyone by false accusation I will restore fourfold," **verse 8.**

Zacchaeus found his own treasure chest filled with silver, gold; the works! He offered half of his riches.

> "And Jesus said to him, today salvation has come to this house, because he is also a son of Abraham; for the Son of Man has come to seek and to save that which was lost." **Verses 9-10**

A song writer penned, "Love Lifted Me". Jesus delivered me from the sinking boat. The widow's husband passed away, but she kept on singing, "Just do what the LORD Say Do." She could leap up and touched her toes even at eighty years old; living on in great company at its best. This reminds me of a great comedy, *The Golden Girls*, which we loved to watch many years ago in fact some of their films are reviewed to date it is recorded.

"He that is faithful in that is least is faithful also in much: If therefore you have not been faithful in the unrighteous riches, who will commit to your trust, the true riches**?" Luke 16:10-11.**

In Him, faithfulness pays great and wealthy benefits. He said:

"And if you have not been faithful in that which is another man's, who shall give you that which is your own? No servant can serve two masters: for either he will hate the one and love the other; or else he will be loyal to the one and despise the other, you cannot serve GOD and mammon." **Verse 12-13**

It's a choice; a give and take back world. Yet beware. Satan works online year round and never alone says.

"Now the Pharisees, who were lovers of money, also heard all these things. And they derided Him and He said to them: You are those who justify your selves before men, but God knows your hearts. For what is highly esteemed among men is an abomination in the sight of God." **Luke 16:14-15.**

Jesus made it plain even today in parables says.

"There was a certain rich man which was clothed in purple and fine linen, and fared sumptuously every day. And there was a certain beggar named Lazarus who was laid at the gate full of sores desired to be fed with the crumbs from the rich man's table moreover; dogs came and licked his sores." **Vv 19-21.**

Good, verses bad; regardless what we think we will reap what we sow;

> "So it was, the beggar died was carried by the angels into Abraham's bosom. Then the rich man also died and was buried: In hell he lifted up his eyes being in torments to see Abraham afar off, Lazarus in his bosom. The rich man also died and was buried," **verse 22**.

Already damned, he thought he could take his wealth to hell.

> "Then he cried and said, Father Abraham, have mercy on me and send Lazarus that he may dip the tip of his finger in water, and cool my tongue; for I am tormented in this flame. But Abraham said son remember in your lifetime you receive your good things, likewise Lazarus evil things, but now he is comforted and you in torment." **Verse 24-25**

My mind is set on our Father's interview. Imagine being face to face with Jesus. Suppose He asked, although He read my mind to the core of my heart, when, where, what, why, and how do I know warrants were issued to warn his brothers a way to escape life in hell?

> "Then he said, I pray therefore, father that you will send him to my father's house, for I have five brothers that he may testify to them, lest they may also come to this place of torture. Abraham said to him they have Moses and the prophets let them hear them." **Verses 27-29**

Awesomely, Jesus humanized the rich man.

"But He said to him, if they do not hear Moses and the prophets, neither will they be persuaded though one rose from the dead." **Verse 31**

Jesus, the great Examiner and Explorer will fix it all. Heartfelt reality entered within a hit song; says "Yes God Is Real."

Remarkably, a journalist interviewed a little boy three years old when he preached his first sermon. The reporter asked him who his teacher was. Because, his mom said she wasn't a public speaker, and his dad was bashful. So the reporter asked the little boy seven years old at that time who taught him to preach? As a result, the little boy said he first prayed and then read the lesson. So he held the message in his memory, since it was the God in him. The reporter asked him if he would be a pastor of his own church, but he wanted to be a doctor to help little children. The reporter asked who his favorite Bible character was. He answered Daniel. I remain flabbergasted.

He spoke great things; only God released to him by Him. After all, Daniel dared to stand up for God. Key verses glorified Him. During his youth he described a way God reacts to him saying:

"He reveals deep and secrets things; He knows what is in the darkness, and light dwells with Him. I thank You and praise You, O God of my fathers, You have given me wisdom and might: And have made known to us the king's demand," **Daniel 2:22-23**.

A former classmate's daughter had a five year old son, who said God talked to him when he was alone. I asked her what age has got to do with the God in us. Absolutely nothing! Jeremiah is a witness. He wrote:

> "Then the Word of the LORD came to me saying: Before I formed you in the womb I knew you; before you were born I sanctified you, I ordained you to be a prophet. Then said I Ah, LORD God! Behold, I cannot speak for I am a child." **Jeremiah 1:4-6**. He made his case: "But God said to me: do not say I am a child: For you shall go to all to whom I send you." **Jeremiah 1:4-7a**.

Jeremiah received his God given assignment. Abruptly He declared:

> "And whatever I command you, you shall speak: "Do not be afraid of their faces: For I AM with you to deliver you says' the LORD. Then the LORD put forth His hand and touched my mouth, and the LORD said to me:" and he believed Him in action when God said. "Behold I have put My words in your mouth, See I have this day set you over the nations and over kingdoms to root out and pull down, to destroy and throw down, to build and to plant;" **vv 7b-10**.

> Amen!

The interview revealed God talked to Jeremiah who was awed-inspiringly in His divine will. His will be done, seen in **vv 11-14,** as He promised;

"For behold, I Am calling all families of the kingdoms of the north, says the LORD; they will come and each one his throne at the entrance at the gates of Jerusalem against all the wall of Judah." **V 15** continues **vv 16-18** to be continued: I looked down saw away to escape evil things we should know God said to Jeremiah: "They will fight against you, but they will not prevail against you, for I Am with you, says' the LORD to deliver you," **verse 19**.

To make these things plain to us, my dear readers, we are included, because I turned the pages over to the New Testament and read today what Paul wrote:

"Oh, the depth of the riches both of the wisdom and knowledge of God: How unsearchable are His judgments and His ways past finding out. For who has known the mind of the LORD? Or who has become His counselor? Or who has first given to Him and it shall be repaid?" **Romans 11:33-35**.

A writer wrote, "I can't pay the LORD: But I can thank Him."

"For of Him and through and to Him are all things, to who is glory forever Amen." **Verse 36**

For example,

"Jesse made seven of his sons pass before Samuel. And said to Jesse, The LORD has not chosen these. And Samuel said to Jesse: Are all the young men here? Then he said there yet remains yet the youngest and there he is, keeping the sheep." **1st Samuel 16:10-11**;

Imagine a breakthrough, while quietly keeping sheep.

> "So he sent and brought him in. "Now he was ruddy, with bright eyes, and good looking and the LORD said Arise, anoint him; for this is the one!" **verse 12**.

Spiritually, In God we trust Him, the Word is nothing but the absolute truth!

> "Then Samuel took the horn of oil and anointed him in the midst of his brothers; and the Spirit of the LORD came upon David from that day forward. So Samuel rose and went to Ramah," **verse 13**.

God is known for miraculous miracles, written to understand God is still calling His people.

> "Now Samuel did not yet know the LORD, nor was the word of the LORD yet revealed to him. And the LORD called Samuel again the third time. So he arose and went to Eli and said here am I, for you call me: Then Eli perceived that the LORD had called the boy." **Verses 7-8**

The results manifest graciously great blessing. I stick to a song titled, I believe, "When I Woke up this Morning I Had No doubts." God is infinite. He has no end or beginning, but one thing I know; number seven shows out for Him with purpose.

> "Now the sixth month the angle Gabriel was sent by God to a city of Galilee named Nazareth, to a virgin betrothed to a man whose name is Joseph of the house of David." **Luke 1:26**.

God's great and mighty blessings are beyond measure.

> "The virgin's name was Mary. And having come in, the angel said to her, Rejoice highly favored one, the LORD is with you, blessed are you among women!" **Luke 1:27-28**

I've heard, save the best for last. Who so ever is destined from the beginning is purposely set apart in Him.

> "But when she saw him, she was troubled at his saying, and considered what manner of greeting this was. Then the angel said to her: Do not be afraid, Mary, for you have found favor with God. And behold, you will conceive in your womb and bring forth a Son, and shall call His name JESUS." **Vv 30-31**.

Amazingly, favor may not be fair, but God introduced Him.

> "He will be great, and will be called the Son of the Highest; and the LORD will give Him the throne of His father David. And He will reign over the house of Jacob forever, and of His kingdom there shall be no end. Then Mary said to the angel, how this can be since I do not know a man." **Vv 32-34, Mary was p**urposely destined, always the virgin mother of Jesus

> "And the angel answered and said to her, The Holy Spirit will come upon you, and the power of the Highest will over shadow you; therefore, also, that Holy One who is born will be called the Son of God. Now indeed, Elizabeth your relative has also conceived a son in her old age; and this is the sixth month for her who is called barren." **Vv 35-36**

What's age got to do with love; young or old?

> "For with God nothing will be impossible: Then Mary said, Behold the maidservant of the LORD! Let it be to me according to your word. And the angel departed from her." **Verses 37-38.**

A song writer wrote, "Let It Be Dear LORD Let It Be." The psalmist confessed truthfully, great things I know. So let go and let Him.

> "God is our refuge and strength, a very help in trouble. Therefore we will not fear though the earth be removed, and the mountains be carried into the midst of the sea though the waters thereof roar and be trouble, though the mountains shake with the swelling thereof." **Psalm 46:1-3**:

The sons of Korah trusted God, who is available to help everyone always. Clear like the water we must have to drink, as well as use immeasurably, for we cannot make it without water.

> "There is a river whose streams shall make glad the city of God: the holy place of the tabernacle of the Most High. God is in the midst of her, she shall not be moved; God shall help her, just at the break of dawn. The nations raged, the kingdoms were moved; He uttered his voice, the earth melted." **Verses 5-6**

Now earthquakes happen, yet,

> "The LORD of host is with us, the God of Jacob is our refuge. Come behold the works of the LORD. He makes wars to cease to the end of the earth; He

breaks the bow and cuts the spear in two; He burns the chariot." **Vv 7-8**

The psalmist hit the nail on the head in likeness of the One nailed to a cross.

> "Be still, and know that I AM God; I will be exalted among the nations, I will be exalted in earth! The LORD of hosts is with us; the LORD of Jacob is our refuge," verse **10**.

My grandson, sixteen at that time, questioned my belief in God, yet he accepted Jesus as his Savior years ago. I invited him outside and asked him to look up at the sky. Then I asked, did man form the sky or the cool breeze that blew across our faces. He was speechless. A Mighty Fortress Is He. A look of wonder shined in his eyes, confirmed God works wonders.

In memory of a friend and woman of God, there is a song recorded within her eulogy which she passed on to me, and I passed to her wonderful family. Within it reads:

> "I will lift up my eyes to the hills, from whence comes my help. My help comes from the LORD, which made heaven and earth. He will not allow your foot to be moved; He who keeps you will not slumber." **Psalm 121:1-3**. To be continued: "Behold He who keeps Israel shall neither slumber nor sleep. The LORD is our keeper, the LORD is your shade at your right hand. The sun shall not strike you by day or the moon by night: The LORD shall preserve you from all evil. He shall preserve your soul. The LORD shall keep your going out and

your coming in from this time forth, vv 4-8a
moving on I copy a part two true story saying "and
even forevermore." **Verse 8b**.

During our youth, one day we reached a turning point in the
middle of a lake, with about five of us on a boat. We
couldn't swim. We cried out to God and He rescued us.

> "Jonah prayed to the LORD his God from the fish's
> belly and he said I cried out to the LORD because
> of my affliction; and He answered me. Out of the
> belly of hell I cried and You heard my voice,"
> **Jonah 2:1-2**.

Nothing is better than God when He is on our side. Even
so, Jonah tried to escape God's assignment. And I got it,
because it is fact checked. Nothing is too hard for God. I
face many hard times being an elder, but God is my stay.
An unnamed writer summed it up just right, for the young
and old.

> "Therefore we also, since we are surrounded by so
> great a cloud of witnesses, let us lay aside every
> weight and sin which so easily ensnares us, and let
> us run with endurance the race that is set before us;"
> **Hebrews 12:1**

It is the same as a certain young lady who went through a
storm. Her husband passed away. She had two young
beautiful daughters. The oldest, full of life in Christ,
completed college and worked with young people. God
called her name and she passed away. Her singing mother
continues to worship God in songs and prayers. The young

lady didn't seem to look right or left. She was 'Looking to Jesus.' Storms come and go.

Then the same psalmists' made a case for all whosoever believes is going through down time in the hall of fame on earth.

> "For consider Him who endured such hostility from sinners against Himself lest you become weary and discouraged in your souls. You have not yet resisted to bloodshed striving against sin and you have forgotten the exhortation which speaks to you as to sons:" **verses 3-5a**.

If the shoes fit wear them:

> "My son do not despise the chastening of the LORD, nor be discouraged when you are rebuked of Him. For whom the LORD loves He chastens," **verses 5a-6a.**

As a result, instantly a song stuck in my mind; "My Soul Loves Jesus". A young woman, I believe, loves Him. God always pulls her up with the help of others. A couple of sisters in Christ help anyway the wind blows, because 'it's the God in her', is her personal testimony.

> For "Great is the LORD, and greatly to be praised in the city of our God, in the mountain of His holiness. Beautiful for the situation, the joy of the whole earth is mount Zion, on the side of the north; the city of the great King. God is known in her

palaces for our refuge. For, lo, the kings were assembled, they passed by together." **Psalm 48:1-4**.

God willing, my books continues in Him.

November 30, 2008, my two granddaughters' ages seven and nine, begin to argue after church. I talked to them in regard to their character towards each other. Afterwards we had prayer; all was good. Before we reached their street, the two begin to argue again. Suddenly, I made a left turn on that street. A truck hit us on the passenger side. My oldest granddaughter screamed her leg was hurt. I leaped out of my truck and tried to open the door. It failed to open. So I ran around to the driver's side; opened my door they jumped out safely. Then I called out to the other driver to see if he was okay, but, he very angry yet he stood on both feet safe.

A man who witnessed the accident called the police. I was ticketed by a police woman to appear in court. All I could think was the four of us were safe from all hurt, harm and danger, because both trucks were totaled out. To God be the glory. I pray before leaving home; offered praises to Him. To my surprise a senior citizen informed me when she had a wreck, the first thing the judge asked, when the last time her eyes were tested. I got the message sent from heaven, I made an appointment had my eyes tested.

Fervently, I prayed every day before my court date. I arrived in court and sat quietly; listening to people make their cases before the judge. He began to get very frustrated with some people, whether true or false I didn't know. He locked some up on site.

Then it was my time to face the Judge. I stated my name, age and address. He asked how I managed to look twenty years younger than he. I said judge, your honor; I do a whole lot of praying. He said I figured you were going to say that. Then I added, praise the LORD of glory it pays to praise Him. The Judge laughed out loud, as did the people in his courtroom. He checked my police report; asked honestly how do you know the wreck was your fault? I responded judge; your honor, a police lady ticketed me not the other driver. He said that do not mean you were the guilty one. He shocked me being so kind to someone like me.

Actually it felt like Christmas in the city of my hometown. The judge looked straight in my face, asked have you been charged with a wreck that was your fault? I said no sir judge; your honor. He said I will not put this report on your record. Then he asked how long has it been since your eyes were tested? I smiled and said Judge; your honor a few days ago. He asked was it before your court date? I said, yes sir judge; your honor. He laughed out loud again, as did the people in his courtroom.

 Inspiringly, a thought stuck in my spirit in the judge's courtroom; it is Jesus. In honor to God, the judge, he accepted the truth in that place. The judge ordered me to pay a 30.00 dollar court cost; watch a movie for safety; then ordered me to go home and have a very Merry Christmas,

As a result, the judge's attitude changed before all the people right in his courtroom. He showed the people favor a week before Christmas Day. Whether the driver was charged or not, who knows? I found out four things about the other driver; he had no drivers' license, nor was he a citizen of the United States. He didn't speak English, or the owner of the truck he drove.

God is our refuge He spared us. It could've been me a long way from home in a foreign courtroom, with a guilty plea over my head. But instead, there were no charges, except court fees. Jesus made a way for all of us to escape death as a result. The judge rewarded me, because I told him the absolute truth, he dropped my charge. I will remember that judge's tender loving kindnesses' to an old widow who prays to God favorably, for He is my refuge and highlight of my life!

A young man, very close to my heart, was riding with me in my truck, said respectfully; I bet you think about this left turn every time you turn on this street. As a result, I spoke from my heart. I said not only this street, in respect to our God. I realized, whether turning left or right He reminds me to stay focused in Him; 'Less than our best is failure'.

 In my conclusion, as results, I write absolutely the truth. A lady who works on many court cases was present that c day. She passed on. Never had she seen the judge act so kind-hearted; especially to a senior citizen sixty-five years old, favorably. An unnamed psalmist man or woman, said as it is written, shows character-wise, a way to win.

> "Let your conduct be without covetousness; be content with such things as you have. For God Himself has said, I will never leave you nor forsake you. So we may boldly say: the LORD is my helper; what can man do to me?" **Hebrews 13:5-6.**

Jesus said; "Heaven is My throne and earth is My footstool." A taste of **Acts 7:49a**.

Solomon said:

> "All the rivers run into the sea, yet the sea is not full; to the place which the rivers come, there they return again. All things are full of labor; man cannot express it. The eye is not satisfied with seeing, nor the ear filled with hearing. That which has been done is what will be done, and there is nothing new under the sun." **Ecclesiastes 1:7-9.**

I believe God.

> "My hand has made all these things?" "But Simon Peter answered Him LORD, to whom shall we go? You have the words of eternal life. Also we have come to believe and know that You are the Christ, the Son of the living God." **John 6:68-69**.

His disciples got it; Jesus, the Son of the living God. The longer they lived in His presence, they knew Him. One out of twelve was a devil. He failed to see great rivers running to and fro into one river.

Solomon recorded:

> "They shall fear You as long as the sun and moon endue, throughout all generations. He shall come down like rain upon the grass before mowing like showers that water the earth. In His days, the righteous shall flourish and abundance of peace until the moon is no more." **Psalm 72:5-7.**

God said, in the year of 2010, to someone like me; Obamacare, the Affordable HealthCare Act, will prosper In Him.

Find Jeweline Andrews on Facebook:

www.facebook.com/JewelineRAndrews

www.ingramcontent.com/pod-product-compliance
Lightning Source LLC
Chambersburg PA
CBHW060754050426
42449CB00008B/1398